PRAISE FOR

Living for a Living

"Have you ever hoped that life was about so much more than just survival or more than just living to make an income? Reading *Living for a Living* is like someone handing you a cup of cool water after wandering in the desert. In the movie *The Matrix,* the character Morpheus offers an invitation, 'You take the blue pill—the story ends, you wake up in your bed and believe whatever you want to believe. You take the red pill—you stay in Wonderland, and I show you how deep the rabbit hole goes. Remember: all I'm offering is the truth. Nothing more.' Jamal shares a perspective which lays the groundwork for a new mindset. If you choose wisely, you'll begin living life from a different paradigm than what culture has tragically hammered into all of us. Such a timely and helpful book. One of the most important books I've ever read."

BOBBY DOWNES
FOUNDER OF CHRISTIANCINEMA.COM AND CHIEF
STRATEGY OFFICER AT GIVING COMPANY

"Jamal has an incredible ability to weave stories and concepts in ways that will help you reframe your reality. And when you reframe your reality, your dreams can come true. This book is not just advice, it is not just directions and how to's. This book is the challenge to our norms and change to our perspectives that we all need. Sit down, open your heart as you open *Living for a Living* and expect your life to transform."

LUCAS GIFFORD
LIFE COACH AND PODCASTER

"Solid gold! All coaches sprinkle nuggets of wisdom into their advice and *Living for a Living* is no exception. There are take-aways and lessons at every turn—but this book went even further. As Jamal carefully explained how to move from an attitude of scarcity to truly live, I got the feeling that every word in this book was chosen very carefully and it made me want to read it slowly so that I didn't miss a single thing. That is exactly what I did, but it was so compelling that I still finished it in one day. I couldn't put it down! You won't be disappointed."

KARL FOREHAND
LIFE COACH, AUTHOR, AND FORMER PASTOR

"Jamal is to the self-help industry what the electric guitar was to music. This revolutionary book will be an earworm of inspiration for those who seek to dance to the tune of sacred goals—not from a place of frazzled grit, but from one of presence and love. Buy this book immediately and plan to make it an annual read!"

MEGGIE LEE CALVIN
AUTHOR OF *THE BLUEBONNET CHILD* AND DIRECTOR OF ENGAGEMENT AT THE INSTITUTE FOR DISCIPLESHIP

"Jamal Jivanjee has done it again. Following his brave and groundbreaking first release, *Free to Love*, Jamal now tackles another stronghold in our culture and in the minds and hearts of its people—work, and specifically, working for money. For far too long, our society has sent a false message that what you *do* defines you, and that money is god—the ultimate source of happiness and freedom. Jamal deftly explores and offers a redefinition of work, money, exchange, time, and fulfillment in *Living for a Living*. I can't recommend this thought provoking, paradigm-shifting work enough."

BRANDON CHASE
WRITER AND PODCASTER, BRANDONCHASE.NET

First Edition

Cover design and layout by Rafael Polendo (polendo.net)

ISBN 978-1-938480-38-6

This volume is printed on acid free paper and meets ANSI Z39.48 standards.

Printed in the United States of America

Published by Quoir
Orange, California

www.quoir.com

JAMAL JIVANJEE

Dedication

This book is affectionately dedicated to Amelia Joy. May the work of your divine heart and hands create a home of safety, peace, and love for the most vulnerable and precious of creatures on our planet.

Acknowledgements

The gratitude that I feel for my parents cannot be adequately expressed with words. The struggle of my father (growing up in East Africa and desperately seeking a better life in America) and my mother (faithfully working a government job she hated for over thirty years) has afforded me the greatest luxury that I could ever ask for in life. That luxury came in the form of a critical decision that I made at an early age: I decided that I would not live the life they lived. Instead of a constant struggle to survive, I would live for love. Their sacrifice was the foundation for my paradigm-shift, and it's upon their shoulders that this book is written.

I would also like to thank the magnificent Sousa family. Their love and acceptance of me at a critical time in my life also cannot be adequately described with words. When I think of home, I am reminded of a place where I am fully seen, accepted, and celebrated. The Sousa family has been this to me like no other. This book could not have been written without them.

I would also like to thank Rafael Polendo and Quoir publishing for their constant encouragement and support of my work. I'm convinced that the one thing that makes Quoir the best publishing company in the nation is the fact that it is not merely a business, but a family made up of genuinely synchronous relationships. This is priceless. As an author, there is no other publishing house where I would want my work to reside.

A special thanks to the members of our focus group (Craig Arledge, Jennifer Cowles, Christy Fike, David Fox, Samuel Grissom, Kévin Hude, Vincent Oliveira, and Alyson Sousa) for their careful review of the manuscript. The analysis and insight they provided are worth more than gold.

Lastly, I would be remiss if I didn't thank myself for never believing what society and other well-intentioned people told me about success, money, and what to do for a living. My determination and commitment to follow my heart has made all the difference. Without the rock-solid courage of my own convictions, I could not live for a living.

Table of Contents

Foreword

Religion is too often in the afterlife business, and for Christians, Jesus is significant because he is the one who punches your ticket to heaven. There are two inescapable facts of the human situation. First, every single one of us is going to die. Second, not everyone will truly live. The tragedy is not the former but the latter. We don't need help dying. The problem is that we know not how to live...fully, wholly, unreservedly, bravely, authentically, unapologetically. Or as William Wallace said, "Every man dies, not every man really lives."

Insert Jamal Jivanjee.

Jamal is living. Not just existing. Anyone who knows Jamal, knows this about him. His moment of enlightenment was discovering the truth that we are not born into this world to go to work, pay bills, wait for heaven, and die. We are here to live completely, in all respects. Our chief vocation in life is to live, hence his title, *Living for a Living*.

Jamal isn't the first or only one to have discovered this. Henry David Thoreau uncovered this truth in the woods and wrote,

> "I wished to live deliberately, to front only the essential facts of life, and see if I could not learn what it had to teach, and not, when I came to die, discover that I had not lived. I did not wish to live what was not life. I wanted to live deep and suck out all the marrow of life, to live so sturdily and Spartan-like as to put to rout all that was not life."

The human saga over the course of history isn't just a story of surviving, but one of thriving. Maslow's Hierarchy of Needs identifies "self-actualization" as the highest aim of every human person—to realize our fullest potentialities and possibilities in life. The experience of being fully alive.

Maybe we are not human beings having a spiritual experience, nor spiritual beings having a human experience. Maybe we are human beings experiencing being alive. But what does this really mean? In *Living for a Living*, Jamal shows us how being alive includes: deep feelings of love and belonging; peak experiences of beauty and transcendence; profound human encounters of solidarity and compassion; occurrences of transformation in the crucible of hardship and adversity; exhilarating experiences of inhabiting our uniqueness; operating in the flow of our natural gifting and passion; expressing ourselves authentically and fully; and moments when we perceive all things put together and whole.

One of the colossal errors of the Christian church has been telling people that the relevance of Jesus is fundamentally about what happens when we die. Jamal writes, "One of the great disservices that American Christianity has afflicted upon our perception of the kingdom of God has been the preoccupation with the afterlife."

Jesus himself said, "I have come that they may have life, and have it in all its fullness." This is one of the bedrock convictions behind *Living for a Living*. Jamal writes, "I'm convinced that the good news doesn't just apply to some realm in the afterlife after we die, but has relevance in the day-to-day life of our present existence."

As an author and professional writing coach, it's rare that I find a book that is uncommon and extraordinary both in the message and content, and the faculty and skill in which it is written. Jamal is a masterful story-teller. His writing is enlightening and compelling. He has that rare gift of communicating profound truths in the simplest of terms. There's a striking clarity and penetrability to this book, which is paramount to the gravity of the subject.

With each chapter, Jamal invites the reader into a new possibility of engaging life on different terms. It's not a book you have to labor through; it's the kind of book you don't want to put down. His tone is spiritual but not religious. It is also practical as he deconstructs the dominant cultural views about money, work, consumerism, gender paradigms, family, social justice, and building a world that works for everone.

I am a spiritual director who has worked with countless people who were damaged through their involvement in fundamentalist Christianity, and left it all behind. There's an unfortunate aspect of this because they were taught a distorted view of God and Jesus by the church. Jesus is often the poster-child for a regrettable Christianity, but that's not his fault. I wonder about the impact it might have had if they could have understood Jamal's Jesus and read his book, *Living for a Living*.

Make this book about you and your life. Now is the time to get serious about if and how you're living. You have to decide what to do with the time you have been given. You cannot wait any longer. Whose life are you living anyway? Is it really your life, or a default life based upon the beliefs, mindsets, narratives, ideologies and expectations that have been programmed into your head? Decide right now that you are going to live your life differently. Weigh every paragraph and chapter of this book against the question of your life.

Seneca wrote, "Begin at once to live, and count each separate day as a separate life." This is the sense of urgency we must have. The real question is not what happens after you die, but what happens before you do. The greatest courage is not to face death, it is to face life.

JIM PALMER

AUTHOR OF *DIVINE NOBODIES, BEING JESUS IN NASHVILLE,* AND *INNER ANARCHY*

"Blessed is he who has found his work;
let him ask no other blessedness."

—THOMAS CARLYLE

Introduction

The more that folks know about me and my lifestyle, an obligatory question almost always comes up.

"So, what is it that you do for a living?"

My response is usually met with a look of bewilderment and frustration...

"I live for a living."

Most people won't let that response go unchallenged, and since writing has become my perceived profession the last few years, I get this follow up question a lot...

"Do you make enough money from book sales to live?"

"No. My income from book sales is typically very minimal."

"So, what is it that you do for income?"

My response doesn't usually impress them.

"I don't do anything for income."

Sometimes people drop the subject at that point, some-times they find fault in what I have said, and other times they are intrigued and want to find out more. The truth is, however, I don't do anything for income. Sure, I earn some money from book sales, and I also earn money from my personal coaching practice, but this work does not originate from a need to survive. I can't stress the importance of this distinction. My writing and life coach-ing flow from my life's true work which has nothing to do with survival.

I can't say that I have always lived this way, however. There have been times that I have done things strictly for income. But for the last several years, I have labored really hard to resist the pull into that kind of thinking. To be completely honest, it has not been easy breaking out of this mindset. It has been a struggle for reasons that I'm sure you can imagine. It takes money to buy food, and my body requires healthy food on a consistent basis like any-one else. It takes money to travel, and I travel regularly. Basically, it takes money to live in this world. So, as you can see, coming out of the mindset that seeks income has not been a seamless feat.

When I say that I don't do anything for income, I am not saying that I don't work. Actually, quite the opposite. I am always working in some capacity. There was a time in my life that I did not have balance in this area as I obsessed over my work for a variety of reasons. That was when my work was attached to survival and the quest to prove my significance. In this season of my life, however, my work is not a quest to survive or an attempt to prove my worth, but a response to a compelling awareness of love.

CHAPTER 1

Twelve Weeks Early and Infinitely Valuable

As I stepped out of the elevator and approached the doors to the NICU (neonatal intensive care unit), my heart began to race. What would I see? How would I react? The sterile and slightly blinding light of the hospital hallway gave way to the warmly lit and cozily carpeted NICU adorned with rocking chairs, stuffed animals, and nurses whose faces were etched with smile lines of compassion. After carefully scrubbing my hands free of potentially dangerous microscopic monsters that would enter the body of these little ones who were just beginning their journey on planet earth, my daughter and I made our way over to a section of the room that was clearly hers. Personalized cards and gifts from a recent baby shower carefully cordoned off the borders to her son's new home in this world.

Upon entering his cubby, all of our attention was directed toward the center of the room where a little glass cube with two holes in each side stood. Inside the cube was a little mattress and carefully placed lights along with an assortment of wires and tubes. In the center of this little glass cube laid the treasure that was the focal point of it all. As I peered into the glass cube, I saw a precious and delicate little human stretching his tiny arms and legs out in all directions as if he were trying to wake from a prolonged season of hibernation.

Just two weeks earlier, my daughter gave birth to a precious baby boy. He was twelve weeks premature. What a stunning sight it was to behold my daughter shift into motherhood. There is no stronger love than the love of a mother, and it was as if this love was always a part of her. I could tell it was coming from a place deep within. A place that had been there from the beginning.

I was observing a love that was completely pure. It was a love that was filled with desire for another, yet required nothing in return. This little person was barely four pounds and needed just about everything from others simply to survive. This little human being was loved, cherished, and treasured just because he existed. Although the litany of medical professionals and medical equipment was costing tens of thousands of dollars to keep him alive, no one questioned whether this precious gift to the world was worth it. He most certainly was. No one wondered what contribution he was adding to the world. His existence in the world was itself a monumental contribution.

As I observed and pondered this love, a few things occurred to me.

This little person was seen and loved in the way he was meant to be seen and loved. He lacked nothing. He was not viewed as a burden, nor as someone who needed to justify his existence. He was a person of infinite worth, worthy of infinite love, simply because he existed.

Although he was currently seen through those lenses, I was also aware of something tragic that would be communicated to him in his future. At some point in his journey of life, something sinister would be suggested to him—a heinous lie. It would be a lie so destructive that even his very existence would be called into question. This lie would cause the worst kind of blindness. It would be a blindness of identity and self that would expel him from his current state of blissful rest and propel him into a state of perpetual anxiety.

This lie would cause the deepest trauma a person can experience, resulting in a steady flow of "spiritual adrenaline" to put him either in "fight" or "flight" mode. Instead of resting deep within the "self" that is of infinite worth and value, he would begin to run from the trauma. Because this heinous lie would target his very essence— his inmost person—it would no longer feel safe for him to rest in this place of self that once knew no separation from his mother. Once the lie began to spread, he would become aware of another false self. This "false self" would rise out of the shadow cast by the lie and would carry an illusion of detachment and separation.

- This shadow self would be profoundly limited with clearly-defined borders that would perpetuate a sense of separation and isolation from the world around him. Competition with all those close to the borders of his new smaller "self" would ensue.

- This shadow self would be profoundly lacking; taking shape and definition around the desire and pursuit of that which would seem to complete the void within.

- This shadow self would be profoundly unwelcome and homeless. This self would be defined by a continual quest to find a home of his own and justify his own existence. This shadow self would desperately seek to belong at all costs.

This will not be his dilemma alone, as all of us seem to uniquely struggle with self-definition. We attach to labels, symbols, and ideas about who we are as opposed to understanding the reality of who we are. For example, if someone calls you a dog, you might take offense to that. The reason for this is because our identity is attached to the *idea* of being human. If someone challenges your identity as a decent father, mother, or as a productive member of society, you more than likely might become defensive. If you speak to a plant or an animal in this manner, however, you will not get the same response. A plant or animal has no ability to attach to ideas or symbols about its identity. A dog just is. It exists free from the burden to demonstrate that it is a dog worthy of being valued because it is not attached to some idea of what it means to be a dog. It simply *is*. A tree has no agenda of being a good and productive member of the forest. It just *is*.

Can you imagine living your life in this manner? Can you imagine simply being you, as opposed to trying to live up to the concept or belief of what it means to be you? God operates this way. Unfortunately, religions of all kinds are made up of symbols and concepts of what God is and what God is supposed to be, but God is none of these concepts and symbols.

God is *I Am*. Being. Essence. Consciousness. Life. Love.

This too is your source and is the very essence of your being. You are not an idea, concept, or belief. You simply are.

Can you imagine what it would be like to exist as yourself without the need to prove yourself? What would it be like to be *you*, as opposed to striving and working to live up to the idea of who you've been programmed to be?

Yes, like my little grandson, we have quite the ride ahead of us. I am confident, however, that the truth will eventually come out about who we really are beyond the ideas and concepts of what we are supposed to be. It is only from the place of being (*I Am*) where our true work flows.

The quest for survival, however, has been central to human existence for millennia. It's actually been our focus for so long, that any other focus seems idealistic and unrealistic.

I would be remiss if I got too far into this book without introducing my father. Abid Hussein Jivanjee, of Gujarati Indian heritage, was born a British subject on the then-English island colony of Zanzibar located off the shores of East Africa in 1936. Zanzibar, presently a part of the East African nation of Tanzania, was in a precarious position in 1963 when it received its independence from England. Only a month later, the African majority began a revolution against the new government, and considerable violence ensued against the Indians and Arabs that had a long history on the island. Within a few weeks, it is estimated that a fifth of the population had either been killed or fled. Many others who remained endured unspeakable atrocities. My father, along with my grandparents, uncles, aunts, and other relatives, were among those who eventually fled the country to settle in the nearby coastal city of Mombasa, Kenya, on the East African mainland.

Although life in Zanzibar for my father's family (before the revolution) was not a walk in the park, it was stable. Indians were a staple of the local economy and enjoyed a measure of privilege in the British colonial system. When the revolution on Zanzibar began, however, that changed abruptly. After moving to Kenya, my dad's family also faced grim realities. In short order, they went from being

British subjects with many opportunities available to them, to being people without a country. They were no longer welcome in Zanzibar. And in Kenya, they were foreigners without an official homeland.

In Indian culture, the children are raised to eventually care for the family, and my dad began to feel the weight of this responsibility as he became older. After several years in Kenya without discovering meaningful opportunities for a career, my dad's options were pretty slim. His quest to survive and provide for his parents and siblings seemed like an impossible task. As a young single man in his thirties, life seemed to be passing him by, and the pressure to figure things out only increased. They were surrounded by poverty with no apparent hope for the future. This pressure for survival, coupled with the Indian cultural pressure to achieve significance in the eyes of his family, led my father to the edge of a nervous breakdown.

Several years before, in the mid-1960s, my father saw an ad in the local newspaper in Mombasa, Kenya, that was seeking people who were interested in forming pen pal relationships with people from the West. The ad was created by an American philanthropist who wanted to help alleviate poverty in the Third World by connecting people from developing countries with Westerners. Around the same time that my dad responded to that ad, an American woman in her late twenties was working for an insurance company in Columbus, Ohio, sitting in her cubicle when she heard a thirty-second spot on the radio that was seeking people who were interested in finding international pen pals. It was an ad from the same man that took out the ad in the Kenyan newspaper. This woman was seeking to broaden her horizons and wanted to write to someone from India and someone from Africa, so she wrote to the address in the radio ad and was promptly connected to my dad who himself met the two criteria that she was looking for in a pen pal.

This began a thriving pen pal relationship in which they exchanged letters (about two a month) for about six years. Then, when life in Africa looked the bleakest for my dad with no prospects on the horizon, he decided to do something very risky. He proposed to this American woman (whom he had never met) in a letter. She accepted. My dad soon left Kenya, seeking a new world and a new life. On a very limited budget, my dad traveled from country to country, acquiring travel visas as he slowly attempted to make his way to the United States. He eventually made it to West Germany, where this American woman came to meet him for the first time. After this initial meeting, she returned back to the United States to apply for him to come to the States on a fiancé visa.

As you might have guessed, this American woman would eventually become my mother. Growing up in my family was a blend of three distinct worlds: my mother's small-town Midwestern American culture, mixed with the culture and mindset of my father's heritage from India, along with a very distinct African mindset. Each of these cultures are uniquely beautiful, yet they come with significant challenges as well.

As a child, it didn't take me long to see the deep anxiety that my father carried in life. For my dad, survival was the focus of his life in America, as it had been in Africa. Although we lived a comfortable life with everything we needed, I wasn't aware of that growing up. I had the sense that we were destitute and on the verge of winding up on the street. Although this anxiety of mine was not rooted in reality in the least, this was the anxiety that my dad carried, and it deeply affected my life.

Like my dad, I was conditioned to view the world through the lens of lack. Life seemed like a difficult task to endure. To me, living a life just for survival seemed like a cruel joke. Was our existence a problem or burden that needed a remedy? To the world my dad was conditioned by, the answer was "yes." I didn't fully grasp the severity of this mindset of poverty and lack as someone who grew up in the States, but my first visit to East Africa helped me understand the depths of my dad's anxiety much better.

Deep down, I desperately hoped that life was about so much more than survival. Little did I know then, but this hope would become the driving force of my life's pursuit and work.

The good news is this: I eventually *did* discover this new reality worthy of my life's work. My greatest fear has been disproved. I've discovered there is much more to this life than survival. As a matter of fact, our true work has nothing to do with it, because we live in a plentiful universe that beautifully reflects the infinite source that has brought it into being. I could not have discovered this beautiful reality, however, had it not been for my father's deep struggle. It's upon his shoulders that this book is written.

CHAPTER 2

For Sale?

I once conducted a podcast interview with a man who went blind at the age of 47. During our conversation, he said something that I'll never forget. He told me he now realizes, after going blind, that while some things have monetary value, the most valuable things have value beyond money. Then he asked me this: "How much money would you accept for your eyes? Could someone give you enough money to take your vision from you?" The answer was obvious. Some things are invaluable, meaning some things are of infinite value. You cannot quantify something infinite in value with a finite number. Life is of infinite value.

Speaking of life, what is your life worth to you? $10, $20, $40 an hour? For how much money would you be willing to surrender your life?

Do you think you've come to this world just to pay the mortgage, buy groceries, purchase insurance policies, and take a few weeks of vacation each year?

Were you born to live a life preparing for a ten to fifteen-year retirement at the end?

Is the American Dream why the universe exists?

When will you finally have enough money to stop leveraging your life for survival?

Why is love often cited as the most important motivation for life, yet the question of love is rarely contemplated when one considers their work?

These questions deserve careful consideration because we've been slowly and methodically brainwashed for a lifetime of slavery. I don't need to know your personal situation to know this about you. We've all been affected by our societies, families, and religious beliefs. Consider that the average person settles into their careers around the age of thirty. By the time we're thirty, we've been alive for 262,800 hours. That means we've received about 262,800 hours of brainwashing from a global economy based on the need to survive. Obviously, most of this occurs unintentionally at the subconscious level, as survival-based thinking is the fabric of the world into which we've been born.

Think about it, we spend the first twenty years of our lives preparing to work. Then, we spend the bulk of our lifespan working to get to a point where we can retire for the last ten to fifteen years. Then, when we arrive to the golden age of retirement, many struggle to live with meaningful purpose, which greatly contributes to the deterioration of our quality of life before death comes. This perpetual propensity to outsource each stage of life to a perceived future is madness, and it's a waste of life. Nevertheless, each one of us in this life have been given the same treasure. This treasure, where our true life's purpose will be discovered, is contained within the spirit of our consciousness. Spirit and consciousness, however, are only recognized in the present tense.

Unfortunately, most of us live unconscious to the present and to our life's true purpose, and in anxiety, barter away our life's true essence for the purpose of survival. Worse yet, if you've been influenced by Christianity, you more than likely have learned the false virtues of hard work, getting involved in your local church, and earning money to take care of your family. These false virtues (yes, I said false) eclipse the reality of the easy and light nature that exemplified the life of Jesus who told his followers that a radical, new, and long-awaited kingdom had arrived in their midst. This would be a kingdom where the pursuit of survival would be traded for a pursuit of dreams rooted in divine love that dwells in the innermost parts of our being. Unfortunately, it didn't take long for the first-century message of Jesus and this new kingdom to mutate into an idol-based religion centered around the creation of sectarian tribes, the performance of rituals and events, and a preoccupation with the necessities of daily life. Basically, we've been leveraging away our lives to achieve the security of a "normal life."

Paulo Coelho, in his novel *The Winner Stands Alone*, gives us the following list describing a "normal life" that enslaves the world:

- Normal is anything that makes us forget who we are and what we want; that way we can work in order to produce, reproduce, and earn money.

- Spending years studying at university only to find at the end of it all that you're unemployable.

- Working from nine 'til five every day at something that gives you no pleasure at all just so that, after thirty years, you can retire.

- Using Botox.

- Making fun of anyone who seeks happiness rather than money and accusing them of "lacking ambition."

- Believing that art is either worth a fortune or worth nothing at all.

- Despising anything that was easy to achieve because if no sacrifice was involved, it obviously isn't worth having.

- Investing a lot of time and money in external beauty and caring little about inner beauty.

- Believing that other people are always better than you—better looking, more capable, richer, more intelligent—and that it's very dangerous to step outside your own limits, so it's best to do nothing.

- Swearing when in heavy traffic.

- Marrying the first person who offers you a decent position in society. Love can wait.

- Postponing doing the really interesting things in life for later, when you won't have the energy.

- Avoiding depression with large daily doses of television.

- Being equally convinced that aggression and rudeness are synonymous with having a "powerful personality."

This is a far cry from the new world that Jesus proclaimed as good news to the weary and enslaved people of his day. My heart for you as you make your way through this book is that the "normal" life you've been programmed to live would become increasingly unacceptable to you. I hope that as you read this book, the stories of people just like yourself who are transitioning from the economy of survival to the economy of love will whet your appetite to do the same. May this book give you the necessary courage to discover yourself in your true work of bringing heaven to earth. May the eyes of our hearts be awakened to the width, depth, breadth, and height of the love that is ours.

CHAPTER 3

Why?

As I sat in my classroom listening to my teacher read the story, my head began to spin with realization. There was something about the story of the Ant and the Grasshopper that seemed different. This story seemed to grip the very essence of my soul with a deep sadness that only grew as the story unfolded. Day after day, the Ant labored to find, gather, and store up any morsel of food he could find. The Grasshopper, however, would have none of it. Enjoying the summer and attending lavish grasshopper parties would be how he spent his days. Winter was coming, food would be scarce, and the Grasshopper would be sorry. When winter did come, the Ant had plenty to eat. His labors paid off and he would make it through the winter. The Grasshopper, however, was to be pitied. Each year, the Ant labored with intensity to prepare for the scarcity of winter. This cycle would continue over and over for the duration of the Ant's life.

As I listened to my teacher finish the story, I knew it was more than a children's story. I knew it was a story about my dad. My dad was like the Ant. I watched my dad labor each day, diligently storing up money for the scarce winter that always seemed to be imminent. The message of the story was clear: be like the Ant. For me, the message was: *"Be like your dad. Be afraid of the coming winter of scarcity. Work hard to escape it, although you never can. Do this over and over and over again for the rest of your life."*

That day, I came home from school carrying a new sadness that had not been there before. My mother could see it.

Mother: "How was school today?"

Me: "Why does daddy go to work every day?"

Mother: "Because we need money."

Me: "Why do we need money?"

Mother: "So we can eat and have a place to live."

Me: "What happens after he goes to work and gets the money for food and a place to live?"

Mother: "What do you mean? Nothing happens next. That's what life's about. Eventually, we will die."

I felt my spirit sink into a deep chasm. My fears were confirmed. We are just like big ants destined to live a meaningless cycle of gathering and storing so we can survive during the dreaded time of scarcity that always seems to cause anxiety in the adults. I didn't want to be part of this meaningless struggle to survive. I didn't want to live the life my dad was living, but what else is there? How can life be a good thing? It seemed cruel. My mother could tell I was troubled.

"Honey, you're six years old" she said. "You don't need to be worried about such things. There will be plenty of time to worry about this when you're older." Unfortunately, that was exactly what I dreaded.

Many people are taught from an early age to think about what they want to do in life, but this is a colossal waste of precious focus and energy. Before we ask "what," an essential question must come first.

Why?

If we are not clear and conscious about "why," the "what" doesn't matter in the least. As a matter of fact, focusing on answering the "what" question in regard to our career or profession can greatly distract us from the all-important question of "why."

Our society, along with the world and its systems, assumes it knows the answer to the "why" question and then it automatically projects this reason on us as if it's already a given. For the world, the bottom line is survival. This is the world's ultimate "why." In the world's economy of things, lack is reality, so survival is not a given. Whatever is needed for ultimate survival becomes currency, and in our modern era, that is money. Unfortunately, the quest to survive becomes the assumed "why" behind our quest to discover our professions. This is a tragic mistake that I'm convinced we must rectify before we can delve into discovering our true work.

A few years ago, I experienced a season of intense suffering and loss. If I'm being honest, I lost the desire to live altogether. It was the darkest season I have experienced to date. After several months of despair, I developed an interest in looking into people's stories who have had near-death experiences. The more I heard from people who had died and came back with stories of their encounters, the more I experienced a restorative healing. I discovered that no matter what the background of a person was, there were several common elements of these near-death experiences that everyone experienced. People with NDE's (near death experiences) spoke of becoming aware of an unconditional love that went beyond anything they had previously experienced, along with a feeling of being fully home. They also realized that the purpose of this life on earth is centered on discovering how much we are loved, how to receive love, and how to love and serve others.

In addition to this, they were also told that it wasn't their time to stay because their work was not yet complete. Each person had a job to do, and they still needed to accomplish it before their life would be complete. They all returned to this life after their NDEs with no doubt anymore about the "why" of life, even though many of them did not know the "what." They knew that whatever life work they ended up doing, it would have to do with loving and serving others. This is exactly what Jesus said when he gave his disciples the New Commandment:

"A new commandment I give to you; that you would love one another in the same way that I have loved you." (John 13:34)

I'm convinced that the more we awaken to our "why," things will begin to move into place that will lead us into the specific "what" regarding our true life's work. I can tell you from experience that there is a reason why Jesus contrasted the kingdom of the world, whose currency and master is money, with the kingdom of heaven that is governed by another currency entirely. In the kingdom of God, love is the currency. The currency of money and the currency of love can reveal much about the two kingdoms they represent.

CHAPTER 4

The Way or the Guru?

If you've been around Christianity for any length of time, you might think that Jesus's central message was about himself. After all, isn't that what's proclaimed from the pulpits of churches each Sunday? In the evangelical world, the central message is the need to believe certain tenets about Jesus as a life-insurance policy of sorts to prevent his Father (God) from taking his alleged torturous wrath out on humans who deserve to be burned alive because of their sin. If this sounds like a harsh and gruesome message, that's because it is.

Evangelicals will tell you, however, the silver lining is that Jesus was murdered in order to satisfy God's wrath and demand for blood as a ransom payment on our behalf. That message leaves many feeling indebted to Jesus for his kindness in absorbing the blow of his Father's judgement, but it also leaves us feeling unsure how we are to relate to a father who would have subjected us to never-ending torture. This gospel (good news) has hardly been good news for millions who try to grapple with the damaging psychological implications of such a conflicting message. There is more that could be said about that, but that would be another book entirely.

I'm convinced that Jesus's true message to the world was (and still is) undoubtedly good news. I'm also convinced that this good news doesn't just apply to some realm in the afterlife after we die, but has relevance in the day-to-day life of our present existence. You see, we've lost our way. Darkness, torment, weeping, anxiety, stress of living and trying to make ends meet, the fear of not measuring up, the fear of failure, and ultimately the fear of death have been the hell many have been actively perishing in. I'm convinced that the Divine is the remedy to this hell, not the perpetrator of it. The "Way" of Jesus is the solution. I'm convinced it's the good news we've been crying out for in this life, and there is nothing more central to our daily lives than our work and the way we perceive money.

Many of us have forgotten that this universe is plentiful in nature and is a manifestation of the infinite source. Because there is no lack in the source of all that is (God), there is no lack in the manifestation of this source. In a plentiful universe, survival is the last thing that inhabitants need to worry about. The quest to survive runs antithetical to reality. Love is reality, and this love is our truest nature as beings created in the image and likeness of the God who is love.

Much of Jesus's teaching was about painting a picture of this new world governed by a non-punitive, unconditionally-loving God. The power or current (currency) of this new world is love. It's for this reason that Jesus began his public ministry by challenging the economy of lack and money. Talk to any artist, and they will tell you that the concern of money and survival is the biggest killer of the creative process. In marriages and intimate partnerships, one of the biggest causes of breakups is concern and conflict over money. All love and creativity begin in the heart and is imagined in the mind. Both flourish in space free of fear and pressure to survive. This is why creativity, play, and love blossom with the young. To enter into the new kingdom that Jesus is revealing, we must enter into the childlike mindset that exists in us naturally before we are assaulted with ideas of lack and scarcity.

As a matter of fact, the public message of John the Baptist (sent to prepare the Jewish audience of his day for the message of Jesus) was repentance. The English word "repentance" carries a lot of baggage due to religious fundamentalism. This is not different than the religious environment that existed in Jesus's day. The Greek word used in the New Testament that is translated "repent" is *metanoia*, which literally means "a change in mindset," and I would contend that it also means to transcend the mind as well. The kingdom that Jesus came to reveal is built on the foundation of extravagant love, grace, compassion, forgiveness, and relational community that transcends gender, socioeconomic status, and ethnicity.

The old world, however, has been constructed on a scarcity mindset that viewed divine love and acceptance as limited and conditional, a world governed by punitive justice, and a world in which people were kept separated behind the walls of gender, ethnicity, and social status. In order for people to see and accept the radical difference of this new world, an abrupt change in mindset (repentance) would be necessary. This was true in Jesus's day, and it remains just as true today.

When Jesus said, "I am the way, the truth, and the life," the Greek word that is translated as "truth" can also literally be translated as *reality*. If we wanted to gut Jesus's incredible statement into meaninglessness, we would imply that Jesus was speaking of himself as a human individual. A new "guru," so to speak. To project ego on this statement has caused much damage to the message of Jesus in my opinion. Jesus was not setting himself up as the ultimate guru who wanted to start and build a new religion around himself. The "Way" and "Reality" that Jesus embodied goes beyond the two-thousand-year-old Jesus who walked this earth. Even Paul said this in 2 Corinthians 5 when he said that we no longer understand Christ as we once did according to the flesh. The reality of "Christ" is a transcendent "way." If Jesus was simply referring to himself, what does that mean for us? Sure, it sounds good and honoring, but I'm convinced that Jesus isn't driven by ego. He isn't interested in being worshiped as a celebrity. This is the fatal mistake that Christianity makes, and is a major reason why I believe

Christianity has largely been ignorant of the message and "Way" that Jesus manifested with his life. The problem with ego-driven movements is that it disappears with the founder. A quick study of church history will reveal precisely this. In the years that followed Jesus's death and resurrection, the church largely made Jesus into an idol to be worshiped, as opposed to a new Way to be lived and embodied. The Way of Jesus that brought the genders, the ethnicities, and the vast socioeconomic factions of society together, quickly evaporated. Money became king again even within the ranks of the movement that carried his name. It's tragic indeed.

The good news is this: the world can kill a person, but it can't kill a transcendent idea or reality. The two-thousand-year-old Jesus who walked the earth is not physically here today as he was. The Christ consciousness and Way that he manifested, however, lives on through us *as us*. I'm convinced that Jesus is the embodiment of this transcendent reality of fullness that contrasts the old world built upon the illusions of scarcity. In the world of scarcity, money is currency. But in the new world, love is the new economy.

CHAPTER 5

Money, What Is It Really?

"When you get money out of the way, you're allowed to be your best self."

DEAN GRAZIOSI

Money. What is it? Have you ever thought about it? Isn't it weird? Green pieces of paper and metal. Or in modern times, simply theoretical numbers on a computer screen that have value associated to them by a very selective group of people. Seven people to be exact. Even more bizarre is the fact that these little pieces of green paper and metal determine the course of just about everything in our lives. Have you ever thought about where it all comes from? Most of us simply accept the premise of money and its implications for our lives without ever questioning it. It's time we start to question it, however. It is impossible to see into the depths of the new world unless we do.

Again, it's no accident that Jesus began his teaching about the new kingdom by stating that mankind cannot serve both God and money. With that said, let me be clear about something. There is nothing wrong with money. Money is not evil, and it is not wrong to have money. Please don't misunderstand me. However, the idea that mankind must be *preoccupied* with seeking money for clothing, food, and shelter is the very economy of hell on earth that Jesus came to liberate us from. When Jesus spoke of not being able to serve God and money, he was referring to the monetary system which represented an economy rooted in an idea of scarcity and lack which leads to human beings willingly trading their freedom for survival.

It's an economy for slaves.

Although money, in its various forms, has been present since the beginning of human civilization, our modern system of currency in the United States began in 1910 with a clandestine meeting of bankers and wealthy men who were told to arrive at different times so as to not attract attention to the top-secret gathering. The attendees would only use their first names out of fear their plan would be exposed. The meeting was held off the coast of Georgia on Jekyll Island. During this meeting, the men conspired together to write what would eventually become the Federal Reserve Act. Although the men who gathered together were bankers and private individuals, not elected officials, the legislation crafted there was passed on to a congressman beholden to them who then introduced this legislation in Congress to establish a central banking system. Once passed by both houses of Congress, it was signed and subtly passed into law by President Woodrow Wilson on December 23, 1913 when most of the nation was preoccupied with the holiday season. The Federal Reserve began its operations promptly the next year. The Federal Reserve would go on to not only establish the monetary policy of the United States, but eventually, the Fed would go on to lay the groundwork for monetary policy for the international community globally.

Simply put, the Federal Reserve is an agency run by seven board members or governors. This board is not under the direct authority of any government representing any population. With the creation of the Federal Reserve System, the U.S. has agreed to receive its currency from this independent entity. The Federal Reserve determines the value of the currency through its own set of invented standards (rooted in the philosophy of limited supply), and then it prints this currency on green pieces of paper with official-looking markings. This piece of paper is the "Federal Reserve Note" that we call money.

The U.S. Federal Government needs money to run itself, but it doesn't have any currency of its own because it gave its authority to print currency to the Federal Reserve. Therefore, it must now borrow the invented currency from the Federal Reserve. So, the U.S. Treasury prints a certificate on a piece of paper (called a government bond, which acts as a promise to pay back the

Federal Reserve) and gives it to the Federal Reserve in exchange for the certificates that the federal reserve prints on its own green paper (currency). It's not an even trade, however. The Federal Reserve Board charges the government interest for their little pieces of green paper (often referred to as cash) that it prints for the U.S. government. So, even if what was loaned out was paid back in full, there would still be interest owed. Where would the extra green pieces of paper (cash) come from for the government to pay back the Federal Reserve the interest owed? Yes, that's right, it would have to be borrowed from the Federal Reserve yet again, who would then charge more interest for the currency given to the government to pay back the interest on its previous loan!

If this sounds like an insane, self-defeating system, you're right. It's a system designed for perpetual and ever-increasing debt. This sets up a system in which the lender has default authority over the actions of the borrower. This was precisely the point, as this system was designed purposely for the borrower to perpetually be in debt to the lender. It's a system of control and slavery. It's just that simple. It's also important to keep in mind that the government is not some independent entity that is being enslaved. It actually encompasses all those whom the government governs. This system of manipulated currency (that has value because it is limited in supply) is necessary for people to acquire simply to survive. Without this currency, one cannot eat and live and contribute toward the collective debt of those governed under this system.

Mihaly Csikszentmihalyi, author of the best-selling book *Flow*, had this to say about society, which is quite fitting in this conversation:

> "In making us work for its goals, society is assisted by some powerful allies: our biological needs and genetic conditioning. All social controls, for instance, are ultimately based on a threat to the survival instinct. The people of an oppressed country obey their conquerors because they want to go on living."

Because the currency's worth is based upon it being limited in supply, and our biological needs are only available via this limited currency, the threat of not having what we need for survival keeps us in slavery to this system. It's truly a never-ending hamster wheel.

Again, this monetary system of slavery found in our Federal Reserve System is nothing new. Jesus began his ministry by exposing the system of money at its very root.

> "No one can serve two masters. Either you will hate the one and love the other, or you will be devoted to the one and despise the other. You cannot serve both God and money. Therefore I tell you, do not worry about your life, what you will eat or drink; or about your body, what you will wear. Is not life more than food, and the body more than clothes? Look at the birds of the air; they do not sow or reap or store away in barns, and yet your heavenly Father feeds them. Are you not much more valuable than they? Can any one of you by worrying add a single hour to your life?

And why do you worry about clothes? See how the flowers of the field grow. They do not labor or spin. Yet I tell you that not even Solomon in all his splendor was dressed like one of these. If that is how God clothes the grass of the field, which is here today and tomorrow is thrown into the fire, will he not much more clothe you—you of little faith? So do not worry, saying, 'What shall we eat?' or 'What shall we drink?' or 'What shall we wear?' For the pagans run after all these things, and your heavenly Father knows that you need them. But seek first his kingdom and his righteousness, and all these things will be given to you as well. Therefore do not worry about tomorrow, for tomorrow will worry about itself. Each day has enough trouble of its own."
—Jesus (Matthew 6:24-34)

I'm convinced this is the most revolutionary thing anyone has ever said. Hands down. It challenges the very fabric of reality at its root. The quest to acquire money in order to sustain life is the engine of all societies. Its unquenching thirst occupies the consciousness of humanity like nothing else. It is one of the most significant drains on our energy reserves, both individually and as a collective society. Can you imagine a world where survival wasn't our focus? Can you imagine the possibilities that would unfold? Where would our consciousness and focus be in such a world? What would we do? Is this kind of a life even possible here and now?

Yes, it is.

And I propose that we begin actively imagining such a world right now.

CHAPTER 6

The Drawing Power of Desire

"When we adults think of children, there is a simple truth which we ignore: childhood is not preparation for life, childhood is life. A child isn't getting ready to live—a child is living. The child is constantly confronted with the nagging question, 'What are you going to be?' Courageous would be the youngster who, looking the adult squarely in the face, would say, "I'm not going to be anything; I already am."

—T. RIPALDI

"Work is our love made visible."

—KAHIL GIBRAN

When I talk to people about their true life's work, they often are at a loss of what that could be, or even how to go about discovering it. The secret to discovering our true life's work isn't complicated, it's actually something we already know how to do. If you are reading this book, the chances are pretty good that you are a former child.

As a former child, you are an expert at the motivations of childhood. The problem is, we've been so radically distracted from the reality of childhood that it seems like a completely different life. Discouragement, fear, heartache, rejection, comparison, etc...as we begin to experience these things in life, we learn how to disconnect to the vulnerable place of childhood to protect ourselves. This is the beginning of the death of curiosity.

Let me ask you a question, when is the last time you played? Yes, that's right. Played as a child. When is the last time you took the time to daydream? When is the last time you took time to allow yourself to be curious and then to notice what you are curious about?

I'll never forget the conversation I had with the owner of a little coffee shop in my area one particular day. He was an older man who was an accomplished songwriter and artist. He pulled me aside on one occasion and asked me if I knew the meaning of the word "inspiration." I think I gave him some canned definition, and he smiled and told me that he once took a class on how to understand inspiration. I was intrigued and asked him to summarize what he learned about inspiration in that course and throughout his life. What he told me has stuck with me since: *"Inspiration is simply noticing what you notice."*

He went on to explain it this way. Many of us notice things every day. You're standing in line at a coffee shop and someone catches your eye. Maybe it's their expression, or an interaction they are having that you noticed. Maybe you are perceiving their mood or energy, or maybe you're receiving an insight of some kind. Maybe you are looking out of a window and you notice the sunlight illuminate a flower in a particular way and you notice. These moments of noticing happen naturally without any effort on our part. It is part of our nature. These noticing moments are quick moments that are easily overlooked and ignored. While awareness may be a natural phenomenon, noticing what we notice is a skill we must cultivate by becoming aware. My friend went on to tell me that when we learn to take note of what we are already noticing, and to ask why we are noticing something, that's when we learn to live inspired.

For writers and poets, they will write about what they are noticing. Those who sculpt and paint will sculpt and paint what they notice. Teachers will create new and innovative ways to impart the lessons of what they are noticing, engineers will design new processes and systems to arrive at what they noticed, etc...Simply put, childlike inspiration is simply paying attention to the things happening in the present and letting our imagination propel us forward. For many of us, this is a luxury that we think time doesn't allow. I would contend, however, that neglecting this lost art of childhood is robbing us of life itself.

Several years ago, my friend Adriel Johnson began to notice the play habits of his little boy. Much like himself when he was a child, Adriel's son loved to play with Hot Wheels® toy cars and race them on the plastic track that was typical of hot wheel setups. As Adriel observed his son playing, he realized that it was difficult to determine which car won the race because there was no starting or finishing line accessories for the tracks. In that moment, Adriel imagined bringing his son joy by making a Hot Wheel race track accessory. After doing some research, Adriel realized there was no one making these products. Adriel just so happened to be learning about 3D plastic printing during this time, so he purchased a 3D plastic printing machine and made his first Hot Wheel accessory. He made one for his son, and he also made one to sell on the internet. It sold quickly. One thing led to another and Adriel realized that these accessories would sell just as fast as he could make them. They became a huge hit in the Hot Wheel collectors community. This birthed an online business which eventually allowed him to quit his grueling job he was no longer enjoying. Again, all of this occurred because of childlike play. Some of the world's greatest discoveries have come from people who took the time to pursue their childlike curiosity. No, Adriel's life-long dream isn't to make plastic Hot Wheel accessories. His truest desire is to live the kind of life where he could spend the bulk of his time with his kids during their most formative years, as opposed to spending his days away from home as a slave to a job he hated. Amazingly, this is exactly what eventually happened the more he leaned into his childlike curiosity. This brings up a very significant truth that is essential for us to grasp.

THE COMPLETENESS OF A SEED

Some of the tallest trees on the planet are redwood trees. Redwood trees, like all living things, first begin as a small seed. Like all seeds, everything that a redwood tree will become is already contained within the seed. When the seed is planted in the right environment, the seed draws to itself everything it needs to become and grow into what its basic essence is. The same can be said of all of life itself. Did you know that you are a seed? In the same way, when you are planted in the right environment, you also will draw into your life everything (people, resources, knowledge, etc...) that is needed for you to become what you are designed to become. If a seed is sitting in a drawer in your kitchen, however, it cannot develop into its essence. It needs to be placed in fertile soil with water and access to sunlight. The environment in which we sprout, and the environment in which we draw what we need to grow, is actually at the level of our deepest desires located within the core of our being. The more we lean into our genuine curiosity, the more we move toward our desire. The more we live from the place of scarcity and survival, however, the more we are moved away from our core being where our desire is housed. This is tragic as it is our desire that attracts the necessary resources.

CHAPTER 7

Rich Like Birds

A careful observation of the natural world will show us that scarcity is indeed an illusion. For example, let's look at one of the most necessary and plentiful resources needed to sustain life: water. If you ask a person who is living in a drought-stricken place if water is plentiful, they will more than likely tell you no. If you ask a person who is living in a tropical part of the world, however, they would more than likely tell you that water is indeed plentiful. The fact is, there is just as much water on the earth now as there ever has been. The earth's water supply is not being added to, nor is it being used up. If it were, this precious commodity would be gone by now. It simply recycles and redistributes. The earth is mostly water, as it is consistently covered by about 75% water. Liquid water from oceans, lakes, rivers, and streams simply evaporates (by changing into vapor) and form clouds. Clouds travel around the globe and eventually change back into liquid becoming rain. It is through this process that the earth's water supply is redistributed. Even water that is consumed by living organisms ultimately gets redistributed back to the earth through various means. To imply that there is a lack of water on the planet is simply to be ignorant of the bigger picture.

It is for this reason I find it ironic that so many people die annually from a lack of water, and that historically, wars have been fought over water. Of course I do understand that there are shortages of access to water in some places. The supply exists, however, to remedy this issue, and in modern times, so does the technology. The main reason why the problem of accessing water has not yet been solved really has nothing to do with a lack of supply or technical know-how. This issue will be solved when the majority of people grasp that this is not a national issue, but a human issue. The more we realize that separation from one another is an illusion, the more we will realize that there is no *"us* and *them"* and the more we will recognize this as *our* problem and not a problem simply for others. This is an example of just one essential life resource among many we could discuss.

Have you considered the fact that, like water, everything we need to thrive in life in this world is in plentiful supply?

GOD'S SALARY

What is God's annual income? Does that seem like a ridiculous question? It's an important question because it exposes the ridiculousness of the concept of separation.

The answer to this question is both *everything* and *nothing*. God's income is *everything* because the divine is the source and ground of all being. All resources needed for life that emanate from her being are sourced in her infinite essence. This means that God is never separated from any and all resources. Her income is continually everything. At the same time, her income is also *nothing* because nothing is separate from her that she should have need of gaining something outside of her borders.

This is probably not surprising to you as it is not a stretch to think of the divine as being in possession of infinite resources. What is a stretch, however, is to think of *ourselves* in this way. This first dawned on me in a conversation I was having with a friend who was telling me about a job he took that boosted his annual income to the highest level it had ever been. When he said that, I had a realization that a person could only determine their annual income by contrasting it against another. In order to contrast myself with another, there has to be a level of separation. I make one amount of money because you make a different amount, and those can be measured against one another. However, when a married couple calculates their annual income, they typically calculate both of their incomes together as one. This is because marriage is a picture of the reality of oneness. In reality, we are not separate from the divine who is our source. This is why, in reality, we have the same income that God has. Nothing and everything at the same time. The problem with humanity, however, is that we have been blind to true reality for a long time. In our delusion, we have assumed a disposition of separation. As author and theologian Andre Rabe has said: "God is not a being among other beings, but the very ground and source of all being." Nothing exists outside of or separate from being, so nothing in reality exists outside of us.

Since the beginning of human history, however, human beings have been living in an economy of scarcity. This comes from a lens that sees ourselves as inherently lacking in being. It is a deep-seated lie that assumes something is inherently missing from our being which needs to be compensated for. In the Genesis story of creation, this lie was the foundational basis of the serpent's deception of the first humans. The serpent suggested that they *could* be like God if they acquired a secret knowledge they didn't have. The serpent also suggested that God was purposely keeping this secret knowledge from them to keep them from divine likeness. This was a lie because they were *already* created in the image and likeness of divinity. There was no separation between the infinite God (source), and humanity who has their very own being emanating from this source. They truly lacked nothing.

As you are probably aware, the truth of our completeness can seem foreign when all we are accustomed to experiencing are the effects of the lie of lack. When someone feels separated and isolated, they could actually be in a room full of people, and they will still feel alone. Despite the reality that they are not alone, they can only feel loneliness. The greatest fear of humanity is the fear of ultimate abandonment and of being unable to survive. Oh, if we could only see what is real. It's a needless torture that is rooted in the illusion of separation. This plays out in a variety of areas and most acutely manifests itself in our anxiety regarding survival.

Again, Jesus's reference to the wealth of birds is quite significant. *"Look at the birds of the air; they do not sow or reap or store away in barns, and yet your heavenly Father feeds them."* Why are they not sowing or reaping, or storing away resources in barns? Could it be that birds have no sense of lack or scarcity? The birds are intimately connected to the infinite resources of the divine. Not one is cut off from God's awareness or provision. If this is true of simple creatures like birds, could this reality also apply to us? Can you hear the wisdom of Jesus offending our independent human sense of responsibility and security?

LACK MANIFESTED THROUGH EXTRAVAGANT SPENDING AND HOARDING

I have discovered that reacting to one extreme with an opposite extreme is simply another side of the same coin. For example, how often have we heard stories of those whose lives have been marked by extreme poverty, who have come into large sums of money only to spend it all shortly after they get it? Many times, wasteful and extravagant spending can be an attempt to portray an image of wealth to convince themselves or others that they no longer live in lack. Other times, lavish living is the continual attempt to satiate or medicate a perpetual sense of lack.

Another opposite reaction to lack is hoarding. Those who hoard money and resources often do so under the guise of "saving." For example, my dad grew up in an impoverished country where resources were few. He saw extreme poverty in his most foundational years of development. This affected him deeply. As a result, he carried a deep sense of lack his entire life. After he moved to the United States, he began to save money. Growing up, I often heard about how good my dad was with handling money. Although we always had more than enough to survive and live well, my dad was filled with a constant state of anxiety and worry about money and survival. No matter how much we had, it never seemed like enough. As a child, I constantly felt that we were on the verge of bankruptcy as a family, even though that was never even close to becoming a reality.

This brings up a question. When does one actually have enough to stop worrying about not having enough? In my dad's perception, he never left poverty and lack. A person's self-perceived sense of wealth or poverty actually has very little to do with any immediate resources they have in their possession, but in how they view reality. My experience in life has taught me one thing, however, a person's perception of reality often determines their experience. Those who view reality through a lens of scarcity and lack often experience scarcity and lack, and those who view reality through a lens of infinite resources often experience a deep content, rest, and the realization of their needs being met whenever they truly need them to be met.

I'll never forget the time that I saw these two worlds collide with my own eyes during my first trip outside of the United States. I visited a severely impoverished country where I came face to face with real human suffering. I had no grid for this kind of suffering, as I had grown up in the U.S. with relative ease. While in this impoverished country, I spoke with people who were deeply desperate and full of anxiety about their own survival, as you might expect. To my surprise, however, I also met several people who were filled with joy, contentment, and an abundance of peace. These people had a startling lack of anxiety that I was not expecting to see. As a matter of fact, I noticed that they had more peace and less of a concern for survival than people back in the States.

There was one man in particular who was deeply impoverished by any western standards. This man, however, was filled with a joy and contentment that seemed to contrast the understandable anxiety that so many others around him had. He was full of life, and I had to find out why. It didn't take long for me to discover his secret after a few probing questions. He was a local farmer, and his crops had been flooded out that year. He told me he did not know how he would feed his family next week, nor provide milk for his baby in the weeks ahead due to a poor harvest, but with a big smile on his face, he told me that as sure as he knew the sun would rise in the morning, he was confident that he and his family would be just fine. He would worry about tomorrow, tomorrow. He said: "Today, we are all fine."

Today!

That's it, isn't it? Today, not tomorrow. When tomorrow becomes today, there will be enough for today.

Let's come back to our teachers in this area. The birds. Everything a bird needs, a bird has access to. Birds have innate knowledge of how to fly, where to go, where to discover food, as well as an innate drive to build elaborate nests for their young. Birds are never homeless, aimless, or alone. When birds flock together in flight, their beauty and artistry is unmatched. There is a secret to the success of a bird's life, however.

Birds are profoundly undistracted with time the way humans are.

CHAPTER 8

The Art of Surrender

Michael Singer changed the landscape of a major indus-try in the United States from a simple action that began in the woods outside of a small town in Florida. Michael was a bright college student who was on an academic schol-arship studying for a PhD in economics. Everything was going according to plan for him until he made a startling discovery. While sitting on a couch one day with a few friends, there was an awkward break in the conversation leading to a few minutes of silence. Michael noticed that he felt uncomfortable in the silence, but before he could say something, he began to become aware that his mind was racing with thoughts trying to come up with some-thing to say that would fill the awkward silence. What was groundbreaking, however, was his discovery of the one who was observing his racing mind. For the first time in his life, Michael became conscious of a part of himself that he never noticed before: the observer. Who was this silent observer in him that was noticing his noisy mind? How long had he been there?

This experience led Michael down a road to discover this silent observer. It was by taking time to retreat into himself that he began to see how different his racing mind is to this quiet, wise, silent observer. He began to grow a large appetite to get to know this indwelling friend. Could this be his true essence? He was determined to find out. After spending a summer in Mexico by himself learning how to be quiet with his thoughts, Michael was determined that he wanted to spend his life pursuing the inner life. Instead of a lucrative career in economics, Michael decided to pursue meditation, to the consternation of his family and some of his friends. He scraped up what little money he could find and bought a piece of land outside of Gainesville, Florida, where he lived in his van. He was determined to live there in seclusion.

Michael eventually built a cabin on that piece of land and devoted his daily life to pursuing the inner life. This was a profound challenge to him as life's seeming necessities were constantly calling out to him. The more that Michael pursued this lifestyle, the more he realized that all his problems were in the mind which was a prisoner to psychological time. He discovered that the egoic mind cannot exist in the present moment, only in the past or a perceived future. Even if the future that his mind was focused on was only a few seconds or minutes into the future, it was still not present. That's where Michael discovered the root of his suffering.

Michael discovered a life-altering truth through his interactions with the present moment. Everything is just fine in the present moment. Although there may be challenges in the present moment, there are no problems in the present moment. Everything unfolds in the present as it should be, therefore it should be surrendered to. Although Michael wanted to be alone, one by one, people would come and find him and meditate with him. One by one, people also began to want to live with him on his piece of land. This greatly challenged his commitment to surrender to the present. The more he pursued his inner life, the more things like this seemed to unfold.

Despite the fact that he sought seclusion, people kept coming to him. One person in particular wanted Michael to build her a cabin. He just kept saying yes and surrendering, despite the protests of his mind that already had an idea of how his life should be conducted. Others in the surrounding community began to notice the well-built cabins Michael had constructed and wanted to hire him to renovate and add on to their homes. This led to the creation of Michael's first business in the construction industry, which he would eventually name "Built With Love." Michael just keep saying yes to the business opportunities that came his way, and this led to a steady stream of cash flow that he was unaccustomed to. Because he was committed to living a life of simplicity, he took the excess money that he was earning from his construction business and poured it back into his property. This eventually led to more development and construction on his land.

In 1978, a couple of years after the construction company began, Michael walked into a Radio Shack where he saw one of the first personal computers that was made available to the public. He was fascinated with this new device and decided to buy it, although he had no idea why or what he would do with it. He was simply saying yes to the desire that he was observing in himself. After researching the programming manual for a few days, Michael wrote a small program for the computer and showed it to the manager of the Radio Shack store where he purchased it. The manager was impressed with his program and asked him if he would be willing to attempt to write programs for a couple of small medical clinics in the area that he knew were looking for software to help them with their medical practice. There was no software available for the medical industry at that time.

Although Michael was a novice at writing programs (he literally just taught himself how to write a very small and simple program a few days earlier), he continued to surrender to the opportunities that came his way. Saying yes to this opportunity opened the door to a series of events over the next several years that eventually led Michael to create a software package that would go on to revolutionize the medical practice management industry globally. He founded and later became the CEO of a company that would develop into a billion-dollar publicly traded company. Michael's software work in the medical industry is considered so significant to modern history that he and his company's efforts are detailed in the Smithsonian

Institution. Michael's work has spanned four decades, and he has made significant contributions in the areas of education, business, healthcare, and environmental protection. The impact of Michael's life is truly stunning. What's even more stunning is the fact that all of his extraordinary work came from surrender to the present moment. Because of Michael's pursuit of the life within, an extraordinary life and career unfolded that he could never have scripted.

While it is vitally important that we acknowledge and honor the intentions we have for our lives, whenever we hold them loosely and surrender them to the flow of life, we'll discover a rich life that not only encompasses our intentions and desires, but far surpasses them beyond anything we could ever imagine. Like any craft, a life-style of surrender is a work of art that is practiced and perfected in the present.

CHAPTER 9

The Illusion of Time

You have absolutely no problems right now. It doesn't matter who you are and what your situation is. Yes, you're right. I may not know you or your situation, but I think I can confidently say that you have zero problems right now. Think about it. What problems do you really have? If you're thinking about a problem, I can probably predict what kind of a problem you have. As Michael Singer discovered, your perception of the problem is probably rooted in your perception of something that happened in the past, or it is about some aspect of the future that is causing you anxiety because you are uncertain about how something will work. It may even be that you are thinking of a negative situation from your past that you are afraid of repeating itself in the future. All of your problems are rooted in what Eckhart Tolle calls *psychological time*. Psychological time is where the ego resides because that's where fear is, and the ego needs some conflict or war to fight to survive and stay alive. In the present moment, in the state of flow, the ego and false self cannot function.

Right now, as you are reading this, you are breathing. Right now, your heart is pumping blood magnificently throughout your body. At this very moment, you are alive because over thirty-seven trillion cells in your body are performing extraordinary tasks that could be described as miraculous. What problem do you really have at this very moment?

None.

Everything is just fine right now. Again, if something doesn't seem right, it's our perception of the past or of an unknown future that is causing us to feel anxiety.

One of my favorite pastimes is people watching while relaxing over a cup of coffee. I love people watching because people are my passion. I love watching people interact, and I love wondering about their stories. It's probably not surprising that my life's work involves people. I've noticed that I am able to be present with people the most fully when I am not feeling anxious about the future. When fear and worry are absent, our natural passions come into view. Think about it. When do you feel the most free and connected to your passion? Do you even know what your passion is? Being present is essential in this discovery.

One of the great disservices that American Christianity has afflicted upon our perception of the kingdom of God has been the preoccupation with the afterlife. It's is the opposite of what Jesus was attempting to communicate.

Like us, the Jewish people had outsourced their hope into the future when God would establish the long-awaited messianic kingdom. Until then, they viewed their present life as a necessary evil to be endured. Whenever I am talking to Christians about heaven, I love to talk about heaven in the present tense. I love to talk about heaven as something that can be experienced here and now. Not only is this usually met with a "yes, but..." it is often discouraging news to them. This is no different than in Jesus's day as well.

Can you imagine living under the brutality of the ancient Roman Empire, continually hearing about the past glory of ancient Israel under king David and Solomon, or a future day of redemption when the messiah would come and liberate them and restore their glory from the past? Can you imagine the disdain, even anger, when Jesus told them this:

> "The coming of the kingdom of God is not something that can be observed, nor will people say, 'Here it is' or 'There it is,' because the kingdom of God is in your midst." (John 17:20-21)

I recently had this conversation with a friend when their response was along these lines: *"If this is heaven, I don't want it."* While my heart sympathizes with her sentiment, I know that she is only speaking from a perspective that has not yet been awakened to the heavenly world that is all around us. When we let go of the illusion of psychological time, we will find that there is really nothing to struggle against. There is no past to continually re-live, and no future to be resisted or feared. Life is a flow, and trying to struggle against this flow is a complete waste of our creativity and precious life energy. There are always a lot of things happening in the present moment. Even if the moment seems mundane to us.

It's no accident that most of the world's inventors and creatives are folks who have had a lot of "down" time or solitude to dream and create. It's simply the adult version of daydreaming and playing. When I was a child, I could play for hours at a time. I could enter into role playing stories with my friends without thought of what's next. No anxiety about paying bills and survival in the future. No past hurts to dwell on. Just play in the present.

Is it possible to return to this state again? Could this be part of what Jesus meant when he said that the kingdom of God is more suitable for children? What happens when adults learn to be present again like children? Something beautiful happens; we connect with our heart. When we connect with the heart, we begin to dream and create and love. It is through this that true innovation is born, as Michael Singer's life so beautifully illustrates. Inventions, services, and endeavors that serve and better humanity are birthed from this place of present-tense creativity. Trauma from the past and anxiety about the future blinds us to the present tense where life's flow and creativity are found in abundant supply. Ironically, whenever people describe what it's like to experience flow and passion in their work, they talk about becoming unaware of the concept of time. This is essential to the discovery of our life's true work. When we work from flow, "work" ceases to feel like work. It is in this place that we get caught up in the flow where time ceases to exist.

At the end of time, the world will come to an end and a new world will be birthed. The good news is, as soon as we stop seeing life through the lens of linear time (past and future), time will end as we have known it. A new world will be born to us in the present. This world will have no end because it is always *"now."* This is where eternal life, love, and rest will always be found in endless supply. The good news is, this world can be experienced right now, but only at the end of "time."

CHAPTER 10

The Root of Our Evil

It didn't take me long in life to pick up on the message that was being communicated with me: *"Do well in school so you can go to a good college, get a degree in a respected profession, and get a good job earning a decent living."* In the United States, this is how we are taught to sell our bodies in order to acquire money. While the founding fathers of the United States rejected the rule of a monarch in England, we ended up with a tyrannical king after all, despite our best efforts to be free. Money is the real king in the United States.

In Eastern European countries like Romania, the way many sell themselves is a bit different. In one of my extended travels to Europe, I met a young woman who we'll call Katia. Katia was born in Romania, a nation still reeling from the effects of communism and the aftermath of a brutal dictator. Compared to Western Europe, Romania is still years behind economically. Jobs that earn a good wage are difficult to find. So, when Katia was about fourteen years of age, her parents packed up the family and moved them to Italy where there were more opportunities. Katia went to school for a little while in Italy, but after a few years, when she became of working age, she knew what she had to do. She felt that she needed to ease the financial burden that her life was putting on the family. So, Katia dropped out of high school so she could work. There was no work for Katia's parents in Italy, so they moved back to Romania.

Katia, however, knew there was no future for her in Romania, so she decided to stay in Italy. Like so many young girls from Eastern Europe, she had one thing that many employers would find appealing for their businesses. Her body. Many Eastern European girls find themselves working in the service industry as attractive barmaids that bring in customers. Often, many Eastern European girls like Katia end up in some form of prostitution work. As the economy in Italy turned south, Katia moved herself to Switzerland where she found another job as a barmaid. Once in Switzerland, her "boss" gave her a place to live and paid her a small wage. He told her when she had to work and when she was allowed to take time off. Katia found herself working twelve to fifteen hours a day with just a little bit of time to sleep. The longer Katia worked there, the more controlling and intrusive her boss became over her life. Eventually, she was told who she could associate with and where she could go in her little time off. The majority of the money she earns, she sends to her family. This is how Katia proves her significance. This is how many from Eastern Europe are taught to leverage their life for money. It's a modern form of indentured servitude.

In places like Bangladesh, however, many girls are forcibly married off or sold as sex slaves as leverage for money. When a girl is born to a family, she is often seen as a burden, as girls are not able to bring money into the family. They must be taken care of. Girls are not seen as being worthy of being educated past middle school age, so they are sent home and are prepared to be married off to a man who can provide for her. Finding a husband for these young girls is a decision for the girl's father to make as he is the one who is responsible for the financial burden on the family. Many times, the young child bride meets her new husband the day of the marriage ceremony. Many men marry these teenage girls only to later sell them to human traffickers who will offer good money for them.

Troy Anderson, founder of the non-profit organization called "Speak Up" which works with young girls in Bangladesh, has found an effective strategy at combating this grave problem before it even gets started. His organization seeks to ask these young girls this one question: *"What is your dream?"*

While it usually takes time for the girls to understand this question, when they begin to dig deep into their hearts and discover that they actually do have dreams that are *not* tied to survival, everything changes. Girls who get in touch with their dreams almost always refuse the slavery of forced marriage or of being sold as a sex slave. Simply put, girls in Bangladesh who are in touch with their dreams refuse to allow their lives to be leveraged for money no matter what danger and opposition they may face from their families and society. Take a few minutes to let that sink in.

I am convinced that the root of the world's evil can be traced back to the lie of lack that leads to a desperate human quest to survive. This is not just an issue in places like Eastern Europe or Bangladesh. The quest to survive is the foundation of the global economic system that causes us to leverage our lives away as slaves for money. I'm convinced there is nothing more tragic than for a precious life to be traded away for a paycheck. Like the girls in Bangladesh, it is only when we move from a "survival" focus, to a "dream" focus, that we will stop allowing our lives to be sold into slavery.

I recently heard the story of one father who decided that he would protect his children from developing a survival focus. When his children were about four or five years old, he began to tell them that he didn't want them to worry about what they were going to do for money when they grew up. Throughout their childhood, he repeatedly painted a picture of their future for them by telling them that when they grew up, they would always have what they need to survive. He told them if they ever found themselves in need, he would provide whatever they needed. When thinking about their future, he taught them that only one question was important to ask: *What will my contribution be to help make this world a better place?* This is the question that his children were taught to ask themselves repeatedly. Eventually, this man's children grew up and pursued the careers they felt the most passionate about. They got into careers they felt would enable them to best love and serve the world. Incidentally, they are currently well-paid in their professions.

What this father gave his children is truly a priceless gift. To be guided away from a focus that has enslaved the world is the best gift any parent could give their children. Can you hear the heart of the divine speaking through Jesus when he said:

"Don't worry about what you will eat, or what you will wear, for is not life more than food and clothing?" (Matthew 6:25)

This is exactly what is being communicated to us right now. Can you hear this question being asked of you? *Isn't life more than the daily grind to survive? Isn't it more than food, clothing, and shelter?* While we may have never met personally, I can say this with confidence:

There is something in you that makes you come alive.

There is something in you that ignites your passion.

There is something that needs to be remedied in this world that makes you cry.

There is something in you that has been birthed by love.

You might not be aware of these things right now, but that's okay. It's there, buried in the depths of your innermost desires. There is a manifestation of the kingdom of God in you. Discovering that new world in you is what this world desperately needs, and this inner world is where your passion is. The opening of your heart is the key that will unlock all you need in life to live and do your work. This is your profession that is waiting to be unlocked by you. You have been given the keys.

CHAPTER 11

The Myth of Male Provision

After my first two years of general education courses in college, I began to get into the meat of the courses for my field of study. I was a Pastoral Studies major at a large Christian university. In my major, the class sizes were much smaller, allowing me to get to know many of the students in my major. In the beginning of our time together, I met students that were much like me. Students who were eager to make a difference in the world; students who had passion and vision of serving others in some of the most difficult places in our country and around the world. They spoke of feeling led by God to accomplish the seemingly impossible after they graduate, despite the potential risks and unknowns. It was inspiring to be around people with such courage and passion.

As time progressed, however, I began to notice a shift occur in the thinking of many of these students. As they got into romantic relationships and began to think of getting married, money became more of a concern. Where would they live and how would they be able to take care of their spouses and children? As we all got closer and closer to graduation, several of my classmates began to take internships with high-profile megachurches with multi-million-dollar budgets. They began to interview and accept positions with church institutions that offered them great "benefit" packages. The grand dreams and visions of changing the world and serving the underprivileged were spoken of less and less. Five- and ten-year plans were put together that sounded something like this: *"I think I'm going to take the job at (enter religious institution name located in an upper-middle-class white neighborhood in the Bible Belt) so I can save up some money so we'll be able to pursue the vision that God has given me."*

Without fail, after a mortgage, car payment, and a couple of kids, thoughts of giving up the church salary and insurance were unthinkable. The dreams they once had were eventually seen as naive college idealism that were not rooted in reality. Not just that, passages from the bible seemed to validate their new found "wisdom." After all, didn't Paul say that a person who didn't provide for his family is *"worse than an unbeliever?"* This story played out so many times that I lost count. Time and time again, the glimmer of brightness and hope that I once saw in their eyes faded into a sullen fatigue. I knew I had a decision to make. I could settle for proof-texted bible verses that seemed to invalidate Jesus's words from Matthew 6 that liberated us from the world's economy of survival and lack, or I could resist and pursue the impossible desires of my heart despite the economic uncertainties. I decided to do the latter, and it has made all the difference.

Shortly after college, I pursued the dream of planting a collegiate church that I had my heart set on. The only problem was I had to fundraise for everything. I had to fundraise for the church startup expenses, and for my salary, since college churches didn't bring in enough money to support a professional pastor. This did not sit well with some of my concerned family members who thought I should earn a "real" salary since I put the time and money into getting a college degree.

"Who gets a degree for a job that ultimately depends on asking people for money?"

That was the question that came up in family gatherings from my non-religious family. From some of my more religious family and friends, this is what I heard more often: *"Your first priority is to provide for your family. As a husband and a father, God has made you responsible for providing for your family."*

And just like that, Jesus' words about pursuing the kingdom of God and trusting that everything needed will be provided (Matthew 6) was completely nullified. Worse yet, Jesus's words were nullified by other passages of the New Testament. The words of Paul's letter to Timothy were regularly used against those who would seek to be free of the economy of scarcity:

"Anyone who does not provide for their relatives, and especially for their own household, has denied the faith and is worse than an unbeliever." (1 Timothy 5:8)

This passage was a constant source of conflict for me. Every time the bills would start to pile up, I would entertain accusatory thoughts about my life's work and focus. 1 Timothy 5:8 was a very destructive bullet in the gun of the accuser. Finally, I decided to look into the context a bit further and I was stunned at what I discovered.

The New Testament letter of 1 Timothy was a letter that Paul wrote to his friend and co-laborer Timothy who was spending time in Ephesus serving the community of believers there. In that day, if a woman found herself single or widowed, she would need to be cared for, as women were not permitted to have employment on their own accord and care for themselves. As you can imagine, the church community there began to care for the women who were widows. Unfortunately, many people began to take advantage of this. Adult children and relatives of many of the widows who were able to care for their family members instead chose to take advantage of the services of the church community. As a result, the community was becoming overwhelmed and stretched thin trying to care for everyone. Paul's advice to Timothy was to *take care of any widow who has no one else to care for her.* (1 Timothy 5:3)

It was an instruction to help them prioritize the aid to the widows who had no other people to help them. It's pretty straight forward. Paul was frustrated with the people who claimed to be awakened to the love of Christ, yet did not care for their own family members who were starving in their midst. He was frustrated with those who were taking resources from those who really did have need. You can hear Paul's anger and frustration in his statement in 1 Timothy 5:8:

> "Anyone who does not provide for their relatives, and especially for their own household, has denied the faith and is worse than an unbeliever." (1 Timothy 5:8)

Now that makes much more sense. This had nothing to do with seeking first the kingdom of God and trusting that all of our needs would be provided, as Jesus said in Matthew 6:33. Jesus himself lived this way. He gave his life to the fulfillment of his father's business, and he trusted that his needs would be cared for in that process. He even did this when his mother was in his own care as a widow. Have you ever wondered how Jesus "made a living?" We do know that he did carpentry work for a season in his younger years, but what about when he was engaged in his public ministry and traveling? How did he live? How did he eat? We do know there were some women of financial means, like Mary Magdalene, who shared their resources with he and his disciples, but other than that, we don't know the specifics. I actually love that we don't know the specifics. His true work was not about survival and making a living, but about rescuing humanity from a life enslaved to the meaningless task of survival and bringing them back to the place of living from and to love. This was his true work.

THE PRISON

I did not go to college right after High School. My first "real job" after high school was a prison. Literally. I got a job as a corrections officer due to a family connection that pulled some strings for me. I was young and totally unqualified for this job that typically required a college degree in criminology or some experience with law enforcement. I was only a year removed from high school and had zero of those qualifications. It was a high-paying government job with great benefits. Basically, I was locked in a prison for eight hours a day strictly for money. What an appropriate analogy this is for the economy of lack.

I worked at that prison for over four years, but it didn't take me long to know this job wasn't something I wanted to do with the rest of my life. It was actually in the discontent of that job that I began to become aware of a greater desire in my heart. Although I hated my job in the prison at the time, the things I learned there were priceless. I don't think I could have learned the essential life lessons I would need in order to eventually discover my life's true work any other way.

In that prison, I learned that I loved working with people. I loved working with people who were in desperate need of help due to a life of hardship and generational bondage. Some of the things that I witnessed in that prison showed me what the power of love and presence could do in the darkest of places. On the negative side, I learned that I hated controlling people and maintaining the existence of an institution that kept people separated from others. There was nothing natural about seeing a group of people through the lens of their past mistakes and keeping people locked up in cages. I was never able to get used to that. After over four years, I knew I had reached my ceiling as a corrections officer as each day on the job was a battle with overwhelming anxiety. As a result, I decided to resign from that job. It was a decision that many people in my life thought was a huge mistake. Nevertheless, I was no longer willing to stay in that prison simply because of the money or because other people thought I should. I knew my heart longed for something different.

After leaving my job in the prison, I went out of state to attend university with a goal of becoming a pastor. During my time in college, I worked in retail sales, I stocked grocery store shelves on the night shift, and I also was employed at the university as a tutor. I saw these jobs as gifts from God that helped me attend school so I could pursue the dream of being in "full time ministry." Seeing these jobs as being connected to what I perceived as my life's work allowed me to work hard and appreciate the nature of the jobs that I had during that time. I knew they were only seasonal in nature. Compared to my job in the prison, everything seemed light, easy, and connected to the work of my heart.

After college, I planted a church and became a pastor. I had finally gotten what I thought was my dream job. I soon discovered, however, that being a local church pastor wasn't the magic fix for my inherent discontent. Don't get me wrong, there were aspects of that profession that I enjoyed. Interestingly, those aspects happened to be the same aspects of being a prison guard that I also enjoyed: interacting with and helping people. Ironically, the same aspects of being a prison guard that almost destroyed me came right back to the surface after I became a pastor as well. The constant sense of anxiety that I once knew as a corrections officer returned. Like in my job at the prison, in my position as a pastor, I discovered that loving and serving people was secondary to keeping the religious institution intact. As my understanding of God and my desire to serve people grew, those desires began to clash with the bottom line of perpetuating the survival of the machine.

I went to college to study for the ministry because I was convinced that the church was broken, and I naively believed that I could fix it by starting my own. After a few years of attempting to "do it right," I discovered that I had built the very religious institution that I said I didn't want to build. As a result of this realization, I decided to take some time off and travel the world to experience the church outside of the Western American context. I felt compelled to see and experience a reality that went beyond the theological box I had been operating in. I ended up taking a team of twelve people with me on this trip. For several months, this group of twelve people traveled by plane, train, bus, taxi, and foot, through deserts, cities, mountains, and Himalayan rainforests. We made our way through the Middle East, China, Tibet, Nepal, and India. We stayed in hostels on building rooftops, seaside resorts, safe houses in "terrorist" controlled territories, on the floor in tiny apartments, and even outdoors under the stars. During our trip, there were times we did not know where we would stay the night to sleep. What was consistent, however, was the fact that we were together. All twelve of us.

Our exposure to one another consistently for three months became our home as we journeyed through areas that were foreign to us in just about every way. Each one of us was an important part of the team. We looked out for one another and shared our experiences together. We were our home for one another. As we journeyed, we experienced things that stretched us beyond our previous borders of self. We saw one another with our "hair down" so to speak. We got tired together, we got frustrated together, we cried together, and we celebrated together. The only true and consistent shelter that we had for those three months was one another. The people, culture, and experiences we gained were invaluable, but the most valuable part of that trip was the time we had with one another. One of the things that we all dreaded when we returned back to the United States was getting sucked back into our previous rhythms of life. A rhythm that involved working long hours to earn money to pay for our individual lives.

For me personally, I realized that I could not continue working as a pastor in good faith to build a religious institution that I no longer believed in. I had tasted a reality that transcended the machine I had helped build. For me, this meant I needed to step down from my position as pastor of the church I was leading. All the sermons I had previously preached on Matthew 6 were about to be put to the test. "Seeking first the kingdom of God" was now leading me out of my profession that was helping pay my mortgage and medical insurance. At that time, I was married, and I had a young teenage daughter at home. The implications of my decision affected my entire family. It was not a decision that I took lightly. Becoming aware of and following the deep desires of my spirit (the kingdom of God) would now become my new profession and focus. Shedding the myth of male provision was key in allowing me to make this significant change of direction. I had a promise that if I listened to the life within, everything I needed would become available to me in the moment I needed it. For me, the first step was leaving behind a system that could no longer support where my spiritual journey was taking me.

CHAPTER 12

The Beauty of Male Provision

What is the role of the masculine? Years of abuse of male and female gender stereotypes and abuse of women by twisted masculine power schemes have masked the true beauty of the masculine essence. This is especially true when it comes to the beauty of male provision. Although an entire book could be written about the nature of gender and gender expression, I do think touching on the nature of gender is appropriate here in this conversation. In our attempt to correct the imbalances of traditional gender role stereotypes and limitations, I think it would be a mistake to render gender distinctions as nonexistent. The fact is, male and female do exist, and they are not the same thing. While gender is much more than differing genitalia, the genitalia of male and female can be symbolic of how the genders serve and interact with one another. I believe this pattern can be observed in the area of provision.

Author and life coach Lucas Gifford, in a recent podcast teaching on sex with his wife Christa Gifford, expounded on this as he talked about the symbolic nature of male and female genitalia. Lucas states that male genitalia is positioned externally for the purpose of penetration and extension into another, and female genitalia is positioned internally for the purpose of receiving (Episode 14: "Let's Talk About Better Sex," Head to Heart Podcast). I firmly believe that the physical nature of our body is an expression of the emotional and spiritual components of our being. After all, humans are not just physical beings, but also emotional and spiritual beings that are manifested in the physical world. Both genders exist to express a fullness of humanity and divinity through their union and oneness together as each gender expresses its uniqueness in intimate relationship to the other. How a man and woman serve one another specifically may change from relationship to relationship, which prescribed gender roles restrict, but I believe certain gendered principles can be observed nonetheless.

While an entire book could be written about the nuanced essence of the masculine gender, I want to focus specifically on what comes natural for many men who experience a sense of confidence in themselves (often when the father/son paradigm is reconciled and healed) and when they are experiencing a deep sense of love for their significant other. Let me say this about cliché statements and stereotypes: many times, they get developed for a reason. Not all of those reasons are negative or false, even though it is unfair to rigidly box a person or gender into those stereotypes. Things often become cliché or stereotypical because a natural pattern or truth is seen and experienced by many. When the masculine essence is motivated by love and service, it is masculine energy that often tends to be expressed by the desire to earn money and succeed in business to mirror a sense of certainty and security for their spouses and family. This is done from a place of desire and love, not obligation, duty, or fear and anxiety. This traditional masculine motivation can be driven by something much deeper than cultural norms or religious obligations, as this aspect of masculinity can be seen historically in a multitude of cultures and societies. This in no way implies that women cannot be similarly motivated, but could this be why a majority of (certainly not all) entrepreneurs tend to be men? What is it about masculine energy that seeks to forge ahead in the world to provide certainty and security for those they love?

The masculine drive to earn money and provide doesn't always have to be the result of an attempt to survive from a sense of lack, but to serve from a centered place of love. This is especially true when the aim of the man is to serve the world at large, and for this service to also extend to their loved ones. There are countless stories of men who went from unmotivated and destitute, to driven and financially successful, when they were awakened to love. The heartfelt desire to serve and provide security for a family is a well-established drive of the masculine heart that has been liberated from self-defeating beliefs about their own significance. When a man's work is connected to his wider purpose and passion in the world, it's also a true joy to channel this into provision for his loved ones.

I have experienced this personally. I became a father at the age of eighteen and was married at nineteen. At that age, I had recently become a convert to evangelical Christianity and was quickly instructed that my duty as a man was to provide for my family. As a young adult, my entrance into professional work life was birthed from an anxious sentiment of needing to provide for my family from a sense of duty, obligation, and fear of financial destitution. This sentiment actually led me away from the all-important journey that I would eventually need to undertake in order to discover my desires, and eventually, what my true work in the world actually is.

After many years of living from the place of duty and obligation when it comes to earning money and providing for a family, and after going through a divorce, reframing provision around love and service has been a daunting task. Like anything new, it's a process that requires time, courage, and patience. As I have entered a new chapter of my life with a partner, I can say confidently that there truly is tremendous beauty in embracing my masculine essence to serve and love through financial provision.

CHAPTER 13

The Myth of Hard Work

One of the most destructive myths that we've been sold is what I call the "hard work" myth. The essence of this myth is that the key to survival and wealth is a commitment to hard and grueling work. America was largely built by people who had a rock-solid commitment to the hard-work ethic. What gives this myth even more believability is its attachment to religion and the stories of individuals who built successful lives because of their strong work ethic. This myth, however, has kept generations trapped in the hamster wheel of survival and wealth acquisition. Like any compelling myth, the myth of hard work has some truth to it. A wealthy life does involve a life of consistent and diligent work, but if it's truly a wealthy life, the work is not "draining" of our life's essence. More needs to be said about the "easy" nature of our true work, but before we get into that, let's talk about the two kinds of poverty that the myth of hard work produces.

The first kind of poverty that the myth of hard work produces is the poverty of attaining financial security. This kind of poverty is difficult to detect because the lives of these people seem to meet all of the external definitions or benchmarks of what society defines as wealthy. The problem is, however, the motivation for their work revolves around trying to achieve a sense of security that lies just beyond their perceived reach. It's a concept that lives off in the future somewhere. Their commitment to hard work drives them from a place of fear of becoming destitute and a fear of not measuring up to a perceived standard. People who operate with this fear rarely feel that they have left poverty, despite the wealth they may have amassed. Those who live according to the myth of hard work live two *unintegrated* lives. They have a work life, and they have a non-work life. The fact that these two lives are unintegrated is a drain on their life's energy and health. Because poverty seems like it is just around the corner, those who live according to this ethic can ill afford to take time away from their work life. To do so seems criminal and irresponsible. Because of sheer exhaustion, however, vacations become necessary for sanity and rest. It's the exception to the rule, however, and as soon as the vacation is over, it's back to hard labor where health and relationships suffer. It's often at the end of a marriage, other close relationships, or a significant health crisis that the poverty produced by this kind of a life is finally realized. In the end, those who amass great amounts of money in this way usually end up relinquishing it to others who did not labor for it.

The second kind of poverty that the myth of hard work produces is the poverty of those that are financially poor. This kind of mindset pervades much of what is considered the "blue collar" world. Many of these folks grew up in economically depressed communities where factory or hard manual labor jobs were the "secure" jobs people were taught to aspire to. Many folks in these communities never consider any other kind of life because having a "hard work ethic" is the measure of a person's success. To be seen as lazy or unwilling to work hard is ultimate humiliation. This mindset keeps people from asking the deeper questions in life such as, *"Do I feel fulfilled in life?"* or, *"Am I living the life I was sent here to live?"*

These important questions are simply beyond the realm of consideration as the sentiment of *"paying the bills"* is the paramount focus. To the hard-working blue-collar world, philosophical, existential, and spiritual questions are a luxury of the elite or those with the monetary resources that allow them the time to explore such questions. To those indoctrinated by the myth of hard work, their precious energy of life is spent on back-breaking labor simply to survive. Drug and alcohol abuse are often widespread in these communities as a result of a subconscious desire to escape or numb the pain of such an unfulfilled and uninspired life. The myth of hard work keeps people trapped in cycles of hard labor simply for survival's sake, even though there never seems to be enough money.

So, the question needs to be asked, if people discard the "hard work" myth, will this lead to rampant laziness? What exactly is laziness anyway? I'm convinced that there really are no lazy people, there are only uninspired people. I'm also convinced that the myth of hard work creates the opposite of what it wants to encourage either by physically exhausting a person so they can't work and need an escape, or by demoralizing and discouraging a person through a lack of engagement of their heart's true desire. This often leads to uninspired living which is incorrectly labeled as "laziness," as humans were not designed to be slaves to anything or to perform seemingly meaningless tasks.

When I say that the concept of hard work is a myth, I am not saying that inactivity will produce anything. If you are an artist, the masterpiece you are creating will not appear out of thin air. If you are a writer, the book you are writing will not be written without putting your fingers on the keyboard and pressing the keys. If you are an entrepreneur, the company you are envisioning will not be created without your consistent legwork. Over the years, I've had numerous people ask me how I could possibly write a book or write the weekly articles that I wrote when I was a full-time blogger. The prospect of writing to that degree seemed like a tremendous amount of hard work to them. Writing (and now life coaching), although time consuming, has never seemed like hard work to me however. Actually, I don't view what I do as "work" at all. I do what I do strictly for love. I earn an income from my coaching business because it allows me to survive while doing my work. If I hit the proverbial lottery, however, and didn't need to take an income from my work, I would do exactly what I am doing now. When we live and work from love, it truly is like hitting the lottery.

Like anything in nature, when a living organism is aligned with their true purpose, they will function and live the way they were designed. This will be done in a very light and easy way. Have you ever seen a lily striving to be a lily? No, it just is. Have you ever observed a tree struggling to be a tree working to produce leaves and sap? No, it just flows effortlessly from what it is. Have you ever marveled at how well birds are able to soar in the air, and design their elaborate nests? Have you ever observed a sea gull scan the sea from hundreds of feet above, and suddenly dive into the water to catch a fish with effortless grace? Have you ever seen the magnificent hives and honey that bees produce? What about the dams that beavers build? These things come naturally in nature without striving or a commitment to the myth of hard work. Of course, these magnificent works are time consuming and involve a lot of effort, but no debilitating striving is necessary because they are natural expressions of the animal performing these masterful works.

Let's move to people now. Have you ever thought about Mozart's *job*? Can we really say that it was Mozart's *job* for him to compose music? Was it Jesus's *job* to proclaim the kingdom of God? Was it Mother Teresa's *job* to help the untouchables of India die with dignity? Most humans, however, have struggled to love and perform the works of love because of the distraction of survival and the myth of hard work. Again, I'm convinced that people live seemingly lazy or unproductive lives because they are not deeply connected to their true essence. It's in our truest essence and being where God can be found, and it's in this place where our true work is mirrored from the source. It's also important to note that the quality of this work is not exhausting or draining. Remember the words of Jesus:

> "...My Father is always at his work to this very day, and I too am working." (John 5:17, NIV)

> "Come to Me, all you who are weary and burdened, and I will give you rest. Take My yoke upon you and learn from Me; for I am gentle and humble in heart, and you will find rest for your souls. For My yoke is easy and My burden is light." (Matthew 11:28-30, BSB)

God is love, and humans were created to mirror this divine image and likeness through their being. When we are correctly aligned with the flow of love, our life and work will become integrated together as a seamless stream of energy and life. We will no longer live in a dual reality of a work and non-work life. Our work will stream from being, not striving. This will obviously look different for everyone.

You may be asking how you can live this easy life of flow that I'm talking about here. An essential step is getting rid of the hard-work myth. If you'll take an honest look at yourself, you'll see that it hasn't lived up to its promise of a wealthy (fulfilled) life. Recognize that it's a path of poverty. Secondly, take notice of the things which energize you and seem to naturally flow for you. Recognize the things that you would do even if money was not involved. When you discover the flow and passion within you, your work and everything that you need to accomplish that work will be supplied at just the right time. Lastly, it is necessary to discover the wider purpose of how your passion adds value to the lives of others and to the wider world. Seeing this connection is key to keeping your work connected to love and motivated by love. Love is the essential fuel for our work, and without keeping this motivation the front and center of our vision, our ambition often becomes selfish and life consuming.

Becoming conscious of our heart and desires is a journey, however. For many of us, the lies of inadequacy and the assaults against our identity run quite deep. In order to come to a place of rest and peace where the depths of our passions and desires can be accessed, our personal sense of homelessness will have to be addressed.

CHAPTER 14

Selling My Home and Embracing Nakedness

Humanity is made of dirt. Literally. Science has shown us the physical evidence of this. The human body is made up of about 59 elements, and all of them are found in the earth's crust. There is something really beautiful about this picture. Our planet is a sphere of dirt, and this sphere of dirt is our home. We are constructed from the earth, our home. When the divine was revealed to humanity through Jesus, the divine was fully revealed to us as one of us. Jesus was as human as human gets. Like us, he was a man of the dirt. My favorite title or description of Jesus is *"Son of Man."* It was the phrase that he used most often to describe himself.

"Son of Man" is another way of saying *"child of humanity."* It was his way of identifying with us completely. When Jesus said, *"Foxes have holes, birds have nests, but the Son of Man has no place to lay his head,"* I often thought that he was speaking of himself individually. Poor Jesus. Then I realized, he's not singling himself out. He's not operating in self-pity or a martyr's complex. When he said that he's homeless, I'm convinced he was identifying with all of us. As a child of humanity, he felt the struggle that we all feel.

Do we belong?

Where do we belong?

Where can we be so accepted and celebrated that we are able to rest our heads in complete peace and security? Where can we go where our performance or actions cease to determine our acceptance? Where is our true home? Animals are not conscious of this struggle. They simply exist as they were made to exist. Homelessness is precisely a human struggle, and Jesus felt the weight of this struggle.

It doesn't take long for us to realize that we are being pushed out. We've been pushed out to justify our own existence. We've been pushed out to prove that the lie we have been assaulted with, the lie that states we are not inherently significant, and that our existence is a burden, is not true. The fact is, many of us haven't been able to disprove this lie because our identity is directly tied to our ability to exist separately from others. This is the lie that has afflicted us, and like all lies, it cannot be satisfied. It simply must be replaced by truth.

HOME

Home can carry a couple of different connotations. On a positive note, our home can be a place where we are fully welcomed and accepted. A place where our belonging is realized and lived into. On a negative note, our home can be a place of segregation and hiding from others. I believe that much of the unconscious drive to segregate ourselves away from others in our physical dwellings can actually be an unconscious attempt to cover over our own sense of nakedness and shame. Home can be a place to go and hide ourselves from being truly known and seen. Because we have not known our worth and acceptance that isn't tied to our performance, home has become a place to be hidden from the never-ending sense of failure. One of the deepest fears that many of us have is the fear of not having a place to belong. For me personally, however, it was actually through the shedding the clothing of home and getting naked, so to speak, that I found my true home.

We owned a bi-level, three-bedroom home in the suburbs of Columbus, Ohio, when I quit my job as a pastor. This was after my previously mentioned epic trip around the globe that allowed me to see the nature of the institution I had been laboring to build. After some reflection and discussion about the changes this would mean for us, we decided to sell our home. When a couple of friends of ours heard about our decision to sell our home and the reasons why, they extended an offer to us to move into their house rent free. It was a huge confirmation that we were moving in the right direction. Many of our friends and family thought we had lost our minds, however. Most people at our stage in life were buying bigger houses, not selling houses and moving in with people. Although it looked like we were moving in the wrong direction, in reality, we were gaining something invaluable. Time.

We got rid of most of our belongings and put the rest in storage. When we moved into the home with our dear friends, we began to experience life with them. We no longer had to "make" time for this dear couple because we began to share our time with them, and they with us. We also no longer needed to spend enormous amounts of time and energy trying to pay a mortgage for a dwelling that, if I'm being honest, kept us separated from others at that stage in our lives. Life suddenly became much simpler. Like the old adage says, less is more. We spent a year with this precious couple in their home, and I wouldn't trade it for the world. Those memories can never be lost or foreclosed upon. They will be a part of me forever. My love for them expanded in ways that would forever change me and would have never happened had we not had that time together. The moments sitting around the table sharing our hearts, glances, smiles, and tears as we shared life together, those moments are priceless. These things could only have happened in the context of time spent together. I'm convinced that life and love are often overlooked because they happen in the seemingly mundane moments of the present tense. This is where heaven is found, however. The kingdom of heaven is experienced in the eternal present tense of *now*.

To be completely honest, this transition was not an easy one for me. It felt very vulnerable to move into someone else's home after several years of owning our own home. I felt very exposed as it challenged my deep-seated insecurities that I didn't even know were there. Deep-seated lies about being a burden came to the surface. I was forced to ask myself:

"Is my presence in this home with these people a gift to them, or a burden?"

"Do I really belong here?"

"Is my exposure (nakedness) a good thing, or a shameful thing?"

I had to fight through feelings of not being enough. I had to force myself to be present despite the fact that I often wanted to hide in a cave. I had to come to terms about what it is that I truly believe about myself. I became aware of the enormous amount of time and energy that went into maintaining my facade and distance from others. This came from my need to cover my shame and my perceived sense of lack. The problem is, maintaining the mask takes effort and energy that drains us. It is not sustainable. We need a place where we can "let our hair down," so to speak. This is the drive behind the quest of much of humanity to secure our own homes. When you live with people, they see you when the mask cannot be maintained. This is terrifying for those who are not sure of their own glorious identity. For me, when my physical home was taken out of the picture, I was confronted with these fundamental questions of identity. I now had the time and space to explore these questions in the context of relationship.

Eventually I began to see that it was the love I was discovering within myself for myself and for my new roommates, and their love for me, that truly provided me with a place to "lay my head" that year. This was a place where I would be accepted unconditionally. Their home was a mirror of the love and acceptance from within me that was being opened and mirrored back to me. What's ironic is that it took me giving up my physical dwelling to realize that my true home is found in love.

Several years have passed since that glorious season with my friends in their home. I have moved into the homes of others, and others have also moved into my home as well. Life is seasonal, and there are seasons for having a home by one's self or for cultivating family life. I'm not trying to suggest a new rule stating that communal living is a must. It's not. It's a decision that each couple or individual must make themselves. The point I am trying to make, however, is that in a very practical way, sharing daily life with others can limit the hardships of life that many of us attempt to tackle in isolation.

If expenses of the household and of daily life can be shared, that's less time that needs to be devoted to slaving away just to make ends meet. For me personally, embracing a shared life with others has helped me transition away from the economy of monetary acquisition and survival, and into the kingdom of love. As isolation decreases, along with all the practical demands and burdens of life that come with isolation, there will be more time for human connection, relationship, and living. This is the substance of a rich life.

CREATING SPACE FOR OTHERS

After a few years of others extending their home to me, that season came to an end in 2009. I had relocated to the Nashville, TN area, and I was driving back to Ohio to visit family for the holidays when I began to sense God communicate to my spirit. This is how I sensed the conversation progress within me:

God: *Others have opened up their home to you for the last couple of years. You have received much during this season.*

Me: *Yes. It's been such a blessing. I'm so thankful!*

God: *Well, that season is changing. I want you to get an apartment with an extra bedroom, so you can provide* *others with a home for free in the same way that homes have been provided for you.*

Me: *What? Seriously? How am I supposed to do that?*

God: (Silence)

This was exciting, yet deeply concerning at the same time. After I left my job as a pastor a couple of years earlier, my income went down significantly. There was simply no money in the budget for rent. There were zero dollars. Nothing. Nada. Zilch. So, I wasn't exactly sure how I was supposed to go about doing this. In the two years since leaving the pastorate, I had begun a small non-profit organization and was in the midst of putting on a conference. This was more than a full-time job, yet it didn't pay much. I was living out the essence of Matthew 6. I was seeking first the kingdom of God, and my needs were truly being met. Now, it seemed the stakes were being raised. If we were being asked to get a place of our own again, even one with an extra bedroom, would I have to change my focus and look for more income?

When I returned home to Tennessee from the holiday trip to Ohio, we learned that we would need to move from the house we had been sharing with a friend in the next couple of months. This was confirmation to me that we were indeed moving back into a season of having our own place as I had sensed. The two months went by very quickly, however, and we were running into challenges trying to find a place.

We still had no real budget for rent, and my position with the small non-profit that I had started was not being viewed as secure employment by even the most modest of apartment communities. Time was running out for us to find a place. Any place. Honestly, at this point I was not thinking about getting a spacious place to provide others with a place to stay as I had initially sensed we were supposed to do. I was simply trying to secure the smallest and least expensive place for me and my family to live. To make matters more complicated, we were conducting a conference in Kansas City and had to secure an apartment before we left, needing to be out of the place we were staying as soon as we returned. I made the reservation for our moving truck, even though we still didn't have a place nailed down just yet. We decided that if we didn't find a place we liked before we left for the conference, we would stop and apply for the cheapest place we found as we headed out of town on our trip. We identified what our "fall back" apartment would be in case we couldn't find anything else.

We left on a Monday morning for our conference, and we still had not found a place to rent. So, we drove over to the "fall back" apartment community as we headed out of town. They had one apartment available. As we walked through the apartment, I remembered what I sensed back at Christmas. We were supposed to get a place with an extra bedroom, so others could come and stay with us. That would mean we would need a three-bedroom apartment, not the two-bedroom apartment that was the only apartment available. Not only that, the apartment was not good or hospitable for others. This was an apartment for survival, not for hospitality for others. I did not have a sense of peace about this place at all. To top it off, the apartment community manager told us we were not qualified based on our income structure with the nonprofit I was running. We were officially out of options. If the cheapest place in town (which we still could not realistically afford on our budget) turned us down, what other options did we have?

To say that we were stressed out was an understatement. I surrendered. As we drove through a nice suburb on our way out of town, the following three-way conversation ensued between my wife, myself, and God:

Wife: *What are we supposed to do now?*

Me: *I have no idea.*

Wife: *That's great.*

God: *Look over there at those luxury apartments. Jamal, this looks like a nice area that you would really like. Why don't you go there?*

Me: *Yeah right. That's funny. Those apartments are probably more expensive than our previous mortgage back in Ohio. There is no way we could afford that place.*

God: *Think about it for a minute. You don't have $100 a month for rent, let alone $1500. You trusted enough to apply for the low-budget, $500 a month apartment, yet you couldn't afford that. What's your cut off? $600? $750? $900?*

Me: *Let's check those luxury apartments out over there honey.*

Wife: *Are you crazy? The rent on those apartments are probably more expensive that our old monthly mortgage payments were.*

Me: *Let's just have a quick look. We have nothing else to lose.*

Wife: *This is crazy.*

As we pulled into the leasing office, it felt to me as if we drove through a portal into a new dimension. As I stepped out of the car, the air seemed filled with electricity and a vibration of hope and expectancy seemed to be pulsating from my bone marrow. As I walked toward the leasing office, I could hear the accusatory voice in my mind reminding me of the irresponsibility of considering such a thing. I tuned that voice out as I walked into the office. When they asked if we were interested in a two-bedroom or a three-bedroom apartment, I told them we were only interested in their three-bedroom options as I chuckled inside.

When we walked with the leasing agent into the vacant apartment that was available, the first thing I noticed was the light that seemed to permeate every angle. There were so many windows. It felt like home instantly. After the leasing agent finished showing us the luxury apartment, my wife and I had a brief conversation:

Me: *This feels like home. I think this is it! Do you like it?*

Wife: *Of course I love it, but there is absolutely no way we can afford a place like this Jamal.*

Me: *Well, actually, if we're looking at things from that angle, we really can't afford anything at all.*

Wife: *This place is probably more than our old house.*

Me: *Let's get it.*

Wife: *We'll never qualify, and even if a miracle happened and they accepted us, we could never pay the monthly rent. Don't be ridiculous.*

Me: *If this is the place for us, it will be okay. Let's give it a try. This is the first place I've had a sense of peace about and that we both have liked.*

Wife: *Okay, but this is ridiculous.*

We told the leasing agent that we wanted the place. She then told us what the monthly rent was, and yes, it was indeed more than our old mortgage payment. As we filled out the application in the leasing office, we mentioned to them that we worked for a non-profit and did not have the typical pay structure they normally require to prove that we meet their income requirement (which we certainly didn't meet). She relayed the info to her manager in the next office, and they seemed to be understanding. We turned in the paperwork and got on the road to drive to our conference in Kansas City. Just a few minutes later, we got a phone call from them.

They accepted us!

Just like that. It was truly hard to comprehend. We were in utter shock, as you can imagine. We were cleared to move in when we returned from our trip in the middle of the month. We would just need to pay our security deposit and the rent for the second half of the month. We had exactly that much money. So, we turned around and came back to give them the payment for our security deposit and our last two weeks of the month's rent. We paid them, and then signed the lease. That was it. We were now officially broke.

That's when reality set in. When we returned from our trip and moved in, we would need the following month's rent in full in just two weeks! Where would that come from? Did we really just sign the most expensive lease of our lives on a luxury apartment? The inner voice of religious accusation returned.

"You are being a poor steward of your finances."

"You made a rash and unwise decision. You didn't even take five minutes to pray about this."

I again decided to tune out those accusatory voices. I might not have had the logistical answers to where the money for the monthly rent was going to come from, but I did have peace. That's about all I had. I'll admit, it wasn't easy taking my family through this process. My wife didn't have the same peace that I possessed. This weighed on me heavily from time to time. If I'm being honest, I would catch myself falling into anxiety on occasion. The good thing for us was that we had a busy few days planned after we signed the lease. We drove to Kansas City to conduct a conference, and we had no time to dwell on what we had just done. It was after the two-day conference where things got interesting.

We had the opportunity to relax out of state for a few days after our conference before we returned to Tennessee. During our few days off, we received a text early one morning from an old friend, who we'll call Rachel, that we had not spoken with in quite a long time. The text was direct and to the point. There were no pleasantries or the standard greeting that would be customary from someone you haven't spoken with in a long time, it was simply a direct question.

"How much is your monthly rent?"

Obviously, this text got our attention after the lease we just signed a few days earlier. After we texted our friend back with the amount of our new monthly rent payment, there was silence. A few hours later, the phone rang. It was Rachel. The conversation went something like this:

Rachel: *So, I bet you are wondering why you received that random text from me this morning about your rent.*

Wife: *I have to say that I'm intrigued.*

Rachel: *Well, let me tell you the back story. I know we haven't talked in a while, and I don't know what your situation is these days, but I heard something in my spirit while I was driving last week, and it caught me off guard. It was very clear and something I couldn't ignore.*

Wife: *Really? What did you hear?*

Rachel: *Well, this might sound crazy to you, but I heard that I was to pay your monthly rent for the duration of your lease. I didn't know if you guys even have a lease, but I couldn't forget what I heard. After sitting on it for a few days, it kept getting stronger. It was playing on repeat in my mind. So, I thought to myself, "How much could their rent be?" I know how frugal you guys are, so I was expecting a cheap amount. When you texted me back that large monthly amount, I was stunned. That's more than my own mortgage!*

Wife: *I know, it's the most we have ever paid for a place to live too. Actually, we just signed the lease a few days ago, and there is a story behind all of it.*

Rachel: *I'm sure there is, and I don't really need to know about it. When I got your text, I had to sit down and pray and make sure this is what I heard. After doing some more reflecting, I am confident that I am supposed to pay your rent. Although it was more than I was expecting, I make good money for a reason. I guess this is why. So, I want you to know that you can expect a check from me each month in the amount of your monthly rent.*

As you can imagine, when my wife got off the phone and delivered the news to me, she looked like she had just seen a ghost. I was overjoyed and at a loss for words as she described the details of her phone call. I was so glad that she got the news instead of me. It was a huge boost to her faith. The season of time that we lived in that apartment was quite significant, as it became a beautiful place of refuge for several people that needed a haven of rest. The truth is, had we known that our friend was going to be paying our rent ahead of time, we would not have picked a luxury apartment. We would have picked the least expensive place we found. That luxury apartment was exactly what was needed for that season, however, so we had to simply trust our internal guidance as we made the decision to pick that place without knowing the details in advance. The extra bedroom that we had for guests was almost continually filled with people who were trying to relocate to the Nashville area and needed a place to stay while they got their bearings. The divine was communicating to us loud and clear.

"You are my children. You never have anything to fear. I possess all things. So do you. We are one. All you need to do is seek the desires of your heart to love and serve others, and I will take care of the rest. It's in the depths of your desires that you'll find my perfect will. It's in the depth of your deepest desires where I fully dwell."

CHAPTER 15

The Poverty of Ungratefulness

I remember the time I found myself in a small town in the West African nation of Cameroon. I was surrounded by poverty according to Western standards. One evening as I was engaged in conversation with some friends, a man looked me in the eye and told me something that I will never forget.

"I want you to know that there is nothing different about the DNA of African people from the DNA of people from Europe or America. There is nothing different about the soil of the African continent from the soil in Europe or America. The true poverty of Africa is because Africans believe they are poor. Many of us believe we are Third World people because that's what we have been told, but we are all the same. This is just an invented term. We are all human. We Africans simply live out the poverty that exists first in our own mind."

I was stunned to hear him say this. It's one thing for a Western person who lives in relative ease to say this, but for this man to say this was quite profound. This man was not rich by Western or even African standards, but I noticed there was a marked difference with him from many of the people I had met there. He carried himself with a confidence, ease, and authority that many others there did not seem to have. He seemed to live a profoundly non-anxious life. The more I talked to him, the more he told me about the blessings and cultural richness of African culture and people. He spoke as one who is profoundly grateful for all the blessings that he has, and he was not focused on all the perceived things that he seemingly lacked.

There is something profoundly liberating and empowering about having gratitude for the blessings we already perceive that we have instead of being focused on the things that we perceive we don't have. Have you ever felt stuck in life? Have you ever thought "If I just had (insert whatever you perceive you currently lack), my life would be able to move forward?" I know I have. Many of those times, I have actually gotten the thing that I thought I needed and wanted. You know what? It was never enough.

Never.

After the initial excitement waned, I was on to thinking about the next thing I felt like I didn't have. Has this happened to you before? I know many people who seem to be stuck in this kind of thinking, and it leads to a deep pit that can be difficult to climb out of when you're in the midst of it. There are a few characteristics that seem to mark these people's lives:

PERPETUAL CRISIS

If you spend any amount of time with folks in this mind-set, it's like hearing a broken record. You'll hear all about their current crisis and what they need that would remedy the situation that seems to be just out of their reach. Often times, these folks will feel angry at whatever they feel is keeping them from getting what they believe they need. If they come from a religious background, they often become angry at God whom they view as an all-powerful being sitting in the heavens somewhere who is silently looking down at them and refusing to act on their behalf. This view of God is actually part of the problem. Ironically, their anger is also directed at those who are closest to them who have helped them the most.

SHORT-TERM MEMORY LOSS

In addition to being in perpetual crisis, folks who are focused on what they perceive they lack seem to suffer from short-term memory loss. Often, the very thing they believe will solve their problems is something they previously had. They seem to forget that when they actually had the thing or situation they think they now need again, they were in utter despair and were focused on something else they thought they needed. I've known people who were stuck in dead-end jobs who thought their lives would be better if they got out of their job or got a new job. After quitting their job, they began to lament and actually miss the job and the people they once worked with.

I've seen this happen in relationships as well, even abusive relationships. When the abuse is happening, they cried out for help and desired to be free of the abuse. After getting out of the relationship, however, they actually began to miss their former abuser and often ended up right back in the abusive relationship.

I once knew someone who had no transportation and was in need of a car. They thought that if they only had a car, they could get their life in order. It was their missing piece, so to speak. The problem is, when they had a car before, they continually complained about how bad their car was (it wasn't), and how they desperately needed a new one. Ironically, they ended up losing their car in a freak accident. After some time had passed, they got tired of walking and depending on others for transportation. They came to the realization that simply getting any car would be the key to what they now needed in life. How quickly they forgot that they were not happy when they had a car. This pattern of behavior has been happening for a long time. Remember the biblical account of the ancient Israelites? They were slaves in Egypt, and they cried out to God for deliverance from their situation. A short time after they escaped captivity, they lost their memory and began to desire to go back to the very place from which they were rescued. This tendency to forget our recent patterns of discontent keeps us in cycles of bondage by keeping us blind to an internal sense of lack and pain. It also keeps us blind to the blessings we have in the present tense. The poverty of ungratefulness prevents us from moving forward in the vital work we are here to do.

PROFOUNDLY SELF-CENTERED

If you spend time with a person who is ungrateful, you will quickly learn that they have very little capacity to see and focus on others. Their own sense of lack keeps them focused on themselves and what they are struggling to acquire. The only connections they seem to attract to themselves are others who seem to mirror their own sense of lack and ungratefulness, or those who will accept and cater to (enable) their every whim and desire. No matter how much you give to a person who is trapped in the pit of ungratefulness, it will never be enough, and it will never make a dent in their perceived sense of hopelessness. A self-centered person can literally be surrounded by blessings and gifts, yet live in total blindness or indifference to them. They can only identify with and focus on their "false self" that has been built on a victim mentality. When an ungrateful person is focused on the false self built on the illusion of lack, they will not be able to see their true "self" that is in possession of tremendous divine gifts and resources they have been given to affect the world. These essential gifts simply lay dormant and wasted as the ungrateful person desperately seeks to survive.

THE THREE SERVANTS

Jesus tells us a story about this very thing. The parable of the three servants recorded in Matthew 25:14-30 is fascinating to me. Before we get into the essence of this story, I think it's vitally important to remember the Semitic and patriarchal culture of the people that Jesus was speaking to. The stories he would tell are not meant to be taken as a literal metaphor of the divine's exact function with humanity, but instead contain principles that transcend culture and time. This is the case here in this parable, as it was customary in this culture for powerful landowners to have servants do their bidding. It was more of a master/servant type of system where masters had almost absolute control over every aspect of the lives of their servants. It was much more invasive than anything we would experience in our current employer/employee system. The interactions were often heavy handed and colored by a very hierarchical social class distinction. This is important to keep in mind because the details of this parable violate those social norms in a radical way. The notion that a rich master would entrust his servants with all of his wealth without strict guidelines would be unthinkable, and the absurdness of this detail is very purposeful in painting the divine in a very different light than what was being taught by the religious machine of his day. A master's wealth was his very authority and essence. There is a deeper principle at play, and Jesus was communicating this deeper principle of the nature of the kingdom of God within a culturally relevant context.

"Again, the Kingdom of Heaven can be illustrated by the story of a man going on a long trip. He called together his servants and entrusted his money to them while he was gone. He gave five bags of silver to one, two bags of silver to another, and one bag of silver to the last—dividing it in proportion to their abilities. He then left on his trip. The servant who received the five bags of silver began to invest the money and earned five more. The servant with two bags of silver also went to work and earned two more. But the servant who received the one bag of silver dug a hole in the ground and hid the master's money.

After a long time, their master returned from his trip and called them to give an account of how they had used his money. The servant to whom he had entrusted the five bags of silver came forward with five more and said, 'Master, you gave me five bags of silver to invest, and I have earned five more.' The master was full of praise. 'Well done, my good and faithful servant. You have been faithful in handling this small amount, so now I will give you many more responsibilities. Let's celebrate together!'

The servant who had received the two bags of silver came forward and said, 'Master, you gave me two bags of silver to invest, and I have earned two more.' The master said, 'Well done, my good and faithful servant. You have been faithful in handling this small amount, so now I will give you many more responsibilities. Let's celebrate together!' Then the servant with the one bag of silver came and said, 'Master, I knew you were a harsh man, harvesting crops you didn't plant and gathering crops you didn't cultivate. I was afraid I would lose your money, so I hid it in the earth. Look, here is your money back.' But the master replied, 'You wicked and lazy servant! If you knew I harvested crops I didn't plant and gathered crops I didn't cultivate, why didn't you deposit my money in the bank? At least I could have gotten some interest on it.'

Then he ordered, 'Take the money from this servant, and give it to the one with the ten bags of silver. To those who use well what they are given, even more will be given, and they will have an abundance. But from those who do nothing, even what little they have will be taken away. Now throw this useless servant into outer darkness, where there will be weeping and gnashing of teeth.'" (Matthew 25:14-30, NLT)

There are several interesting insights we can glean from this story. First, the servants were not disconnected from the immense wealth of the master. It passed from his hands into theirs with no effort on part of the servants. The amount of resources that the servants received was in direct proportion to their personal strengths. Most scholars agree that it all was a completely lavish amount of money. Even the one servant with one bag of silver was given a lavish amount of money. Again, it was all absurdly over the top which was the point of this story. Next, the master was going away on a trip, and the duration of the trip was the duration of the season of investment for the servants. Reproduction and increase was a natural expectation. Most of the servants understood this. The servants had a tremendous amount of freedom in how they did their work, as there were no rules governing how they were to invest. Eventually, the increase in their master's resources that they invested was passed down to them as well.

The behavior of the servant who buried his master's money, however, was governed by his anxiety of the future, and of his perception of the character and nature of the master. This was a severe deviation from the behavior of the others. None of the servants had any guarantee that their investments would be successful. For the others, the unknown future wasn't a problem, but for the servant who had one talent to invest, the unknown future was a trigger for paralyzing anxiety. He assumed that his master was governed by lack like he was. He assumed his master to be hard and merciless. Could this be the root of his fear? How did he miss the fact that his master literally shared all his wealth with his servants without stipulation or threats? What could have given him the impression that his master was governed by harshness as he assumed? Could this be a commentary on the religious perception of the divine that was, and still is, common?

When you realize that the divine is benevolent, lavish, and good, the unknowns seem less scary.

Renowned life and career coach Mark Peysha says this about anxiety over an unknown future:

> "When you treat the unknown as something that is supposed to be known, you will feel anxious and weak. If you treat the unknown as something you'll work with as you create your options and your future, you'll feel courageous, decisive, and strong." (Mark Peysha, Strategic Intervention)

The question is, what makes a person feel like they have to figure out an unknown future ahead of time? Have you ever felt this way? Why is it that others feel comfortable approaching an unknown future? I have found that how a person views their past is key to how they will approach the present and the future. Let me explain.

IS LIFE HAPPENING TO US OR FOR US?

Every one of us has a past. Our lives are a compilation of what we have experienced. All of us have experienced hardships and endured painful experiences to some degree or another. How we process our history is quite significant, however. How do we view the things that have brought us joy *and* pain? What about our broken relationships and those who have hurt us? What about abuse? While there are no easy answers to these questions, and in no way should we try to excuse or give an overly simplistic reason for the negative things that have occurred in our past, it is important to observe our lives from a wider perspective. Specific things have actually been happening for quite a while. If we look at our life from a bird's-eye view, we'll perceive a pattern. Events and patterns have occurred to us as a way of revealing where we're headed on our journey, and they also show us the obstacles that stand in our way. This is especially true of difficult patterns that we find repeating themselves. We cannot move forward into our purpose and freedom until these "blockages," so to speak, are resolved. This is why difficult situations keep repeating themselves until we overcome them. These blockages are a result of things that we've experienced in our past development and history, and many times they are also connected to the things that our parents (and their parents) have experienced that have been passed down to us. It's all connected, and it's all heading somewhere. Life is happening *for us*, not just *to us*. Everything mysteriously does work together for good as the scripture states. Understanding that life is happening *for us* allows us to accept and perceive the wider story that is unfolding through us.

Understanding that life is happening *for us* and not just *to us* radically changes the way we perceive the future as well. If we perceive our past from the perspective of a victim, our perception of the future will simply be a continuation of the dreaded past. The prospect of this happening is a fear that becomes an unintended focus of ours in the present. Instead of living and sharing the love and life we were meant to share with the world, we become preoccupied with protecting ourselves from a perceived future that could be a continuation of the losses of our past. When we view our present life and future in this way, serving others with our "talents and treasures" takes a backseat to the need of survival. In effect, we "bury" ourselves and the gifts we have been freely given as we simply strive to survive. What we give out of love and service to others grows and multiplies into more, but what we hang on to and bury because of feelings of scarcity and loss, ultimately dies. This is precisely why fear of scarcity and loss lead to scarcity and loss, and feelings of love and abundance lead to the experience of love and abundance.

A huge passion in my life is traveling. I have been traveling both domestically and internationally on a regular basis for the last several years. I recently had the opportunity to take a three-month trip to Europe, in which I hiked the El Camino de Santiago de Compostela (a 500-mile pilgrimage across northern Spain). I also had the privilege of spending some time with friends in France, Portugal, and Switzerland as well. On this trip in particular, I noticed that many of the people whom I spoke with along the way commented that they wished they had the same opportunity to travel and see the world as I did. Some of them told me that their life would be better if they could get out of their stale day-to-day lives they were living. Often, people just see a snapshot of my life and assume there haven't been seasons of struggle, loss, and financial difficulties. I first learned about the El Camino de Santiago pilgrimage several years ago. Through a set of divine encounters, I knew this was a trip I needed take, but I had no idea how that would happen. As a result, I put this trip on the back burner for several years. I eventually went through a very difficult season in life in which I went through a divorce and lost most of my closest relationships and material possessions. Without going through that season of pain and loss, I would never have been in a logistical position to take this epic pilgrimage. My journey on the El Camino changed my life and opened doors that I could never have imagined before I went. The experiences on the Camino led to the healing of issues I had since birth, finding the love of my life, and also to the discovery of the deepest longings of my heart. Again, without the season of pain and perceived loss I experienced previously in my past, I would not have been in a physical, emotional, or spiritually open place to take this trip.

We could see the difficult things that have happened to us, and that still are happening to us, as evidence that we are "victims," or we could see all of our circumstances as ultimately being "for us." What many of us don't realize is that those seasons are just as much a part of the journey as well. It was in those seasons that I learned to see true beauty.

I've come to realize that I don't have to travel to see beauty. I've been learning to see beauty in every place, every person, and in every moment. I've learned to ask myself these questions on a regular basis:

"What will you do with what you've been given right now?"

"Will you appreciate the beauty of all that you've already been given, or will you pursue an illusion of what you think you lack?"

I've discovered this so far in my journey—if we can't appreciate the exquisite beauty in the seemingly mundane places and people already in our lives, no more will be given to us. If we learn to drink in every moment, every place, every person, and cherish all the treasures we have as if we lack nothing, much more will be given to us. Love gives birth to more love, and lack multiplies the illusion of darkness.

Again, the parable of the talents that Jesus told was, in story form, a culturally relevant way of expressing this timeless reality of how our universe was created to work. The servant who was desperately afraid of losing the little talent he was in possession of ultimately lost what little he had, but the servants who let their talents flow without fear received even more. These are the principles of life and love that flow with the source of infinite life and love that gave birth to all of creation. May we understand that our life's essence is the real talent that we possess. When we let this talent freely flow to love and serve others through our passions and work, it leads to life and abundance.

Melody Beattie says it best in this poem:

Gratitude unlocks the fullness of life.
It turns what we have into enough, even more.
It turns denial into acceptance,
chaos into order, confusion into clarity.
It can turn a meal into a feast,
a house into a home,
a stranger into a friend.

CHAPTER 16

It Always Takes a Village

Your body has approximately thirty-seven trillion cells. Each one of these individual cells contains the genetic blueprint for your entire body. Each cell, however, is also a part of a specific tribe of cells that are expressing only a small segment of this blueprint. For example, a skin cell is part of a tribe of skin cells that are only skin cells because their genetic code is only expressing the skin portion of the blueprint of the genetic code that each cell contains. Although the skin cells contain the DNA for the whole body, the rest of the genetic code that is in each cell that does not pertain to skin is actually covered up. It's a laser focus.

This is not only true of skin cells, it's true of all cells from each of the body's systems. Each cell's function is for the benefit and service of the cells in its specific system. Each system then serves the other systems that make up the body. A body is simply all of these microscopic thirty-seven trillion cells working together. Can you imagine if one of those cells changed the blueprint and decided to operate as if it was separate from the other cells? What if that cell then cut off communication with the other cells and tried to be an organism on its own? This would lead to a breakdown of the whole body. If many cells began to do this in mass, it would breakdown the body as a whole. This is precisely what cancer does.

Our first set of "scriptures" so to speak, is nature. The divine has woven the mystery and the profound story of ultimate reality into the very fabric of creation itself. Creation reveals that life is simply a dynamic flow or dance between the individual parts. There is no separation or break from this divine flow that is life itself. I'm convinced that all dysfunction in the world is an attempt to operate as if the parts are separated from the flow and segregated from one another. This is the ultimate lie that leads to a lack of life supply and resources. It begins as a lie in the mind. Then, when it is empowered, it is manifested into the physical world. It leads to poverty, suffering, and eventually death. Violence, war, pollution, and poverty are just external manifestations of the lie of separation and lack that exists first in human consciousness. Jesus exposed this lie when he told his disciples that apart from him, we could do nothing. He was referring to his true nature, the Christ nature. Apart from the divine Christ nature, we could do absolutely nothing. We couldn't even have existence or being itself.

There is a dynamic and divine flow that runs through all of creation that holds everything together. This is precisely what Paul was referring to when he told the church community in Colossae that in Christ, all things exist and are being held together (Colossians 1:17). Apart from the infinite source, there would be nothing. In the same way, a cell that doesn't receive the essence of the body's life from the other cells, or give its life's essence to the other cells it is connected to in the body, either dies or becomes cancerous.

Although America and the West have enjoyed abundant wealth in comparison to the rest of the world, a strong case could be made that the Western ideal of separation and individualism have helped perpetuate the greatest manifestations of global poverty and environmental devastation the world has ever known. When the idea of scarcity is introduced, it causes hoarding and stock-piling by those who have access to resources. A scarcity mindset also causes us to remain unconsciousness to the world around us. Although America is only a small portion of the global population, we possess the majority of the world's wealth and power.

Unfortunately, for the most part Americans are largely unconscious of the suffering around us. When it comes down to goods and natural resources, America actually has the resources to end global hunger and many other of the world's problems. What is lacking is not resources, but consciousness. America is largely unconscious to its connection to the wider world. We are kept unconscious by the illusion of survival as a nation, and this keeps the collective human body from coming together. The vast majority of our national energy is preoccupied with hoarding our power and wealth in the world because of the quest to survive and the fear of not surviving.

This isn't just true of us nationally, it is also true of us on an individual basis. Let's revisit my friend Cindy that I mentioned earlier. According to Cindy, those that pursue their dreams are irresponsible and depend on others to survive. Although Cindy has hated her jobs, she has prided herself on paying her bills without needing the assistance of anyone else. Cindy feels very self-sufficient, and this idea of being self-sufficient keeps her in jobs that she despises. It's a tradeoff for Cindy; she trades her life for the feeling of being "self-sufficient." The question is, is she really "self-sufficient?" I decided to challenge this assertion with Cindy in a conversation that went something like this:

Cindy: *Jamal, I really appreciate your idealism and your commitment to living free from the economy of survival, but it doesn't work. I've seen so many people just sit on their asses while other people bail them out. They bought into this super spiritual belief that if they just pursue their dreams and "callings," everything works out in the end. Well, I have news for you Jamal; that's not how the world works. If it weren't for people like me who actually work 9-5 jobs, who are self-sufficient, and get steady paychecks, people like you wouldn't be able to live as you do and be so idealistic.*

Me: *Cindy, I hear what you are saying. I really do, but I think what you're saying is built on a huge misconception of reality.*

Cindy: *Oh really? I'm the one who is not living in reality? Please enlighten me.*

Me: *Does your employer pay you?*

Cindy: *Yes, of course.*

Me: *Where do they get their money?*

Cindy: *From their customers who pay for the services we provide.*

Me: *So, what would happen if the customers stopped buying the products that your company sells, and what would happen if your company stopped paying you?*

Cindy: *I couldn't survive. I would have to find another job or solution.*

Me: *So, your employer depends on others to buy products, many of which they have to be persuaded to buy through psychological methods of manipulation because they don't really need those items. You also depend on your employer sharing a portion of those funds with you so you can survive. Your employer is motivated to share some of this money with you so you will continue doing your work for them that will allow them to continue producing products* *so they can gain more money. Am I correct about this process?*

Cindy: *Yes, that's how it works.*

Me: *So, your claim to be "self-sufficient" is not really true. You need the customers to buy from your company, and you need your employer to share these resources with you so you can live. That is not that different from people like me who you accuse of not being "self-sufficient."*

Cindy: *How do you mean?*

Me: *Like you, I receive resources from others that allow me to live and continue to do my life's work. Sometimes these resources come in the form of money, sometimes it comes in the form of lodging, sometimes it comes in the form of food or transportation. Like you, those who share their resources with me believe they are also receiving something of value from me, whether they are conscious of this or not. Sometimes the value they receive is some form of encouragement or value from afar strictly through my work, or directly from knowing me personally. That's why they feel compelled to support me and my work in the world. Like you, I am supported by other people. The only difference between you and I is the fact that I am not living under the painful illusion that I am "self-sufficient." To live under that illusion is a painful and lonely existence that isn't even real. None of us are "self-sufficient." All of the natural world speaks to this reality. Consider the rainbow, for example. What is it? It's simply water that is exposed to* sunlight through a certain frequency that allows the spectrum of light to be revealed to our eyes. The existence of the rainbow is interdependent upon the interaction of sunlight and water molecules interacting together. There is no such thing as a "standalone" rainbow floating around in the sky somewhere. Everything that exists has its existence through dynamic interaction with other properties. Physicists have described atoms as literal "events" as all matter is brought into this dimension through friction.

Also, speaking of my work, my work adds true value to the lives of others. It's not an illusion of value that makes it necessary for me to manipulate people with psychological tactics into believing they need something they really don't. Another major distinction between my work and yours is that I am not producing my work in order that I may gain resources to survive, but to love and serve the world. If our work is done simply for our own survival, we're not truly working; we just have a job. To truly live and bring heaven to earth is to be involved in work produced from a dynamic flow that is motivated by love, not survival.

Cindy: *Wow, it seems that I've touched a nerve. You've really been thinking about this a lot.*

Me: *I have. I think this conversation about the economy of survival vs. the economy of love lies at the heart of Jesus's mission to awaken humanity to the kingdom of heaven that is already in our midst.*

CHAPTER 17

The Six Fundamental Human Needs and the Addiction

Renowned life coach Anthony Robbins has done much work in the field of identifying the six fundamental human needs that are found to be consistent regardless of ethnicity, socioeconomic status, gender, age, etc... In 2006, at one of the first TED talks in Monterey, California, Anthony presented the six human needs as the findings of his lifelong work with tens of thousands of people in all walks of life globally. The six essential needs are:

1. Certainty

2. Uncertainty

3. Significance

4. Love and Connection

5. Growth

6. Contribution

Studies have shown that a person who feels they are moving forward in all six of these needs feel like they are living a fulfilling life. We all know of people who have lots of money, yet are still miserable. I would venture to say that a fulfilled life is a truly wealthy life, as true wealth is about much more than money.

For example, without certainty, it literally becomes impossible to focus on anything else. If a person does not feel certain about their very existence, a desperate search to obtain safety becomes a priority over any other human need. If you are in a war zone with bombs falling around you, or if you are unsure if you will be able to survive or eat, you will probably not take the time to read a book in pursuit of personal growth or think about how you can contribute to the betterment of the world.

If, however, you were certain of all things at all times, life would become quite boring and uneventful. As a result, we have a need for uncertainty, change, and creativity. In addition to this, we also have a need to know that our lives have meaning and significance. Because significance is a fundamental human need, the people who feel their lives are insignificant often live uninspired and hopeless. We all have an innate desire to know that our lives are powerful and important at some level. It is typically the essence of parenting to establish a healthy sense of significance to their children. When we receive this, the tremendous amount of energy that many of us expend in life trying to find or prove our significance can be freed up toward our own growth, contribution to the wider world, and connection with others.

Speaking of love and connection, we would not know how to speak, how to walk, how to carry out even the most basic of life's functions (not to mention reproduce as a species), if it were not for our need for love and connection.

Those who feel they lack these four basic human needs will set about trying to fulfill these needs in a variety of ways. Lack, however, is a lie, and a lie can never be satisfied. This is precisely why those who feel they lack certainty, uncertainty, significance, and love/connection will focus on obtaining these needs and will be blind to the last two human needs of self-growth and contribution. This leaves them feeling unfulfilled at a profoundly deep level, as all six of these human needs must be realized for us to live a life of fulfillment. When a person feels, however, that they already have certainty, uncertainty, an inherent sense of significance, and an abundance of love and connection, they will simply look for ways to receive and express these human needs in a non-anxious way as life unfolds around them.

Approaching life from an inherent sense of fullness, as opposed to lack, changes our approach to everything. Instead of desperately looking to fill a void in these areas, we will be able to devote our energy to profoundly enjoying the present life we are living. We will also be able to focus on our need to grow and develop as well as giving back to the world through our life's contribution.

Our understanding and approach to these six human needs greatly affect how we approach our life's work. In Anthony Robbins' research, he has discovered that human beings become addicted to anything that seemingly meets at least three of the six human needs. The addiction in itself is not the main issue, the issue is whether or not the addiction is serving us or destroying us.

ADDICTION

I have a friend whose father is in a very dysfunctional marriage for a variety of reasons. Let's refer to him as Michael. In addition to the many difficulties that Michael and his wife have in their relationship, Michael's wife regularly worries about money and has been very critical of his past career that did not provide the stability or income she felt was adequate. As a result, Michael left his previous profession where he felt a deep sense of purpose to enter another field that his wife deemed as more financially secure.

Michael also comes from a very religious background where maintaining the appearance of a good marriage is a top priority. In addition to that, he struggles with a deep sense of isolation and loneliness. Despite the fact that Michael and his wife don't get along or relate well when they are together, the thought of losing her seems like an unbearable loss for him to bear. Michael knows that not taking his wife's chosen career path would destroy their already fragile marriage. This would of course reflect badly on the good reputation he has earned in his religious circles. Although Michael has been very unhappy with his marriage and work, changing jobs multiple times, he continues to choose to take similar jobs in the same field to please his wife's sense of security.

Why does Michael keep choosing jobs that make him miserable? Because he is addicted. Studies have shown that whatever action seemingly meets at least three of the six essential human needs, becomes an addiction. For example, taking jobs that make him miserable keeps his marriage from imploding. This is perceived as meeting the "connection" need for Michael, although it is simply an image of connection. It's not real. His relationship with his wife is nonexistent. In addition to that, the fact that he has a job with a steady paycheck seems to meet their need for certainty. Also, keeping the status quo going keeps up his image of having it all together in the religious circles that he is associated with. Maintaining this image and identity seemingly meets his need for significance.

For Michael, his sense of lack regarding the human needs of certainty, love and connection, and significance keeps him running in the hamster wheel of life through his addiction to the job he hates. He is desperately trying to obtain these needs by doing something that he has no desire or passion to do. As a result of this, he is distracted from the last two human needs that are essential for a fulfilled life: personal growth and contribution to the wider world around him.

OUT OF BALANCE

I have another friend (who we'll call Andrea) who is bright, talented, and very hard working. Every job she finds herself in, she finds herself being promoted to management positions. The problem is, Andrea hates her jobs and feels trapped by them. I've had many conversations with Andrea to know that she has felt this way for a long time. Not only does she feel trapped by her jobs, she feels very frustrated that she doesn't know what she wants to do in life. Nothing makes her feel inspired and passionate. One question that I like to ask people to help unlock their dreams is this: *If money wasn't an issue, what would you desire to do with your life?*

Andrea despises this question. It elicits an immediate response almost every time. She responds by telling me that this question is not realistic because the need to earn money cannot be separated from real life. To Andrea, "dreams" will not pay the bills, and the people she knows who do pursue their dreams are usually broke. To Andrea, those who pursue their dreams are irresponsible and are usually dependent on someone else to survive. Upon further questioning, however, the concept of *broke* to Andrea is quite rigid. She has been driven in life to not be "broke" like her family was when she was growing up. Financial uncertainty wasn't the only chaotic aspect in

Andrea's family, but it was a major part of it. A sense of a lack of certainty has profoundly shaped her most formative years. Andrea's deep sense of a lack of certainty has propelled her to pursue a life of certainty. Again, whenever we approach life with an inherent sense of lack, it causes us to pursue what we need from *outside* of our being. This is the cause of much suffering. This pursuit runs contrary to the essence of the kingdom of God which is an *internal* reality. Andrea's sense of a lack of certainty has caused her to pursue certainty in a way that has caused her to neglect her other needs.

Every time Andrea begins to dream, her need for certainty causes her to sabotage her dreams with a practical list of pros and cons. When it comes to dreaming professionally and love, a lacking sense of certainty will keep us from accessing our deepest desires in these areas. This is because love and professional dreams actually thrive in the womb of uncertainty and discovery. I'm confident, however, that as Andrea's perspective shifts, she will begin to see that certainty and security is something to be discovered from what she already has. This includes finding certainty in the persistent longings of her hopes and dreams. When this occurs, finding certainty in the present tense (where love and professional desire exist) will not seem like a loss of certainty for her, but an expression of it.

CHAPTER 18

The Great Temptation

I had two instrumental high school teachers that helped awaken me to my life's potential and worth at a pivotal time in my life. One was a history teacher. His no-nonsense yet very personal way of connecting to students was exactly what I needed as a wayward student. I was always compelled by history and humanity, and he helped me integrate this passion into my life in a very personal way. As the years have gone by, my understanding of the impact that Mr. Spitler's history class in the tenth grade has had on me has only deepened. My passion for people and history have since been integrated into my work both on an individual level in regard to helping people understand their own personal history and patterns in their own life's story, and also on a corporate level by addressing how national and international history has affected our beliefs and norms as a society.

Understanding how my passion for human history could be integrated into all aspects of my work has not always been the case, however. Over the years, people who have been close to me have suggested that I would make a great history teacher. If I'm being honest, that thought also crossed my mind as I grappled with the importance of history and how pivotal of a position being a high school teacher can be in regard to impacting young minds.

Several years ago, a couple of friends of mine who worked as teachers at a private school told me their school was looking for substitute teachers, and they thought I would be a good fit for their school. As a result, I decided to take a part-time job there as a substitute teacher. The more I got to know the teachers, the more I became their regular "go-to" substitute. As I got to know the staff and students there, I fell in love with the school. It just so happened that the long-time history teacher for the high school abruptly took another teaching position out of state, and I was approached as a possible candidate to fill the vacancy.

I was quite surprised that I was being presented with this opportunity, as I did not meet the listed qualifications for this position. Nevertheless, they thought that I might be a good person for the job. This created quite a dilemma in me. If there was one job in the world that could possibly lure me away from my current work, it would be becoming a history teacher at the high school level. During that season, I also happened to be going through a very difficult season financially. The prospect of having a more traditional salary seemed enticing to me. When I inquired about what the position entailed, it became clear to me that this job would involve a majority of my time and energy. I knew that the decision I would make regarding this job would shape the rest of my life's work. After some soul searching and conversations with others, including some who saw this teaching opportunity as a perfect solution to my financial struggles, I knew that I would not be able to take this job wholeheartedly. I would be torn between the time this job would entail, and the work of writing and traveling that was the heart of my work at that time.

Making the decision to choose the vocational path that I could embrace wholeheartedly turned out to be vitally important because it helped me anchor this decision internally in my spirit, and not on external circumstances or the opinions of others. Whenever we make an internal discovery that leads us to embrace our deepest desires, it has been my experience that strong obstacles will often arise, circumstantially speaking, for the purpose of integrating our new insight or intention into the practical aspects of our lives. Little did I know that turning down this position would be a challenge to a very real stronghold that had been lying dormant deep inside for quite some time. I realized that the potential of this other career path was actually keeping me from entering into my work wholeheartedly at an unconscious level.

Shortly after I made the decision to decline the position, I entered one of the most challenging seasons of my life. It was in this dark season that I gave birth to my first book.

Although my first book was something that I had been dwelling on for years, it took this dark season of loss to enter into the freedom necessary to write with the dedication and struggle in which it required to be birthed. In addition to that, the life-saving lessons that I learned in this season would eventually give rise to my personal coaching practice. Looking back on this temptation, I can see how this temptation has served as a launching pad for me to discover my true work in writing, podcasting, and ultimately personal coaching. For me, making the transition from the old economy of survival to the new economy of love and service required facing my greatest temptation to date.

CHAPTER 19

Waking Up

"This is the real secret of life…to be completely engaged with what you are doing in the here and now. And instead of calling it work, realize it is play."

—ALAN WATTS

So, how do we wake up from the matrix of survival that we've been immersed in? Is it really possible to live for a living in a world where the illusions of scarcity and lack seem to be manifested everywhere? Is there anything we can do to usher in a new economy where we can be free to actually *live* for a living?

Yes.

As a matter of fact, it's much easier than you may think. For starters, this new economy begins in the realm of our consciousness within. This is what Jesus meant when he said, "the kingdom of heaven is within you." Manifesting this heavenly reality on the earth is an active and ongoing conscious commitment to a series of truths that run contrary to the economy of survival and lack. It is also a commitment to a series of actions that all of us are capable of doing as soon as we finish reading this book. Let's start with some foundational truths of the new world that should be meditated upon daily. Write these down, frame them, and post them in a place where you will see these on a regular basis throughout the day. There is no "Yes, but..." to these truths. They simply are because you are:

- You are not a burden. Your existence is not a drain on resources and wealth. (Stop and meditate on this truth)

- Your existence is a divine manifestation of infinite wealth and value. You are of infinite value. Something of infinite value cannot be measured by a finite measurement. (Stop and meditate on this truth)

- You are welcome here. Your presence is a gift to all who are privileged to know you. (Stop and meditate on this truth)

- You are enough. Your existence and the qualifications inherit in your being are perfect. This is especially true when you are relaxing. (Stop and meditate on this truth)

- You've arrived right on time. You are not late or early. Everything you've experienced has led you to this moment. Everything you've experienced was necessary for you to be aware of what you are aware of right now. (Stop and meditate on this truth)

- You live in a plentiful universe. All the resources that you need in life exist in plentiful fashion. What is currently in your bank account has no bearing on this in either a positive or negative way. (Stop and meditate on this truth)

- You are not separate from other human beings. The situation of the other humans on this planet is connected to your situation, and your situation is connected to the situation of the other humans on this planet. There are no independent individuals. (Stop and meditate on this truth)

- You are here to serve the world with your deepest passions and desires. No one else can do the work that you've been sent here to do. (Stop and meditate on this truth)

Every profession and work, when birthed and motivated by love, is equally sacred and significant. It doesn't matter if you are digging wells in Africa, building homes in the suburbs, making films in Hollywood, planting gardens in the countryside, writing books from coffee shops, serving tables at a local bistro, etc... Love, not salary, determines its significance.

If you're currently in a job or profession that you wouldn't be involved with if it wasn't for the paycheck, don't freak out, but don't settle in either. You have made it this far in the book, which is evident that you are being drawn out of the old economy and into the new economy. No matter how bleak you think your situation currently is, there are signs of your true calling there. Observe your duties at work and take notice of what ignites even the smallest sparks of intrigue and excitement. In addition to your job, observe what brings you a sense of purpose in life itself. What work would you love to be involved with if you had no need for money? Pay attention to your daydreams.

BECOME A TIME TRAVELER

If I could tell you one thing that some of the happiest and successful people on the planet do on a regular basis, would you be interested? Studies have shown that most people who struggle with depression tend to dwell on painful thoughts from the past or anxious thoughts about a future that they are afraid of. What if you could travel forward in time and see where you *desire* to be in one year? They key word is "desire." Where do you desire to be in love and in your work life? What does it look like one year from now? Don't let your mind remind you of the obstacles to get there, just see it as if it were already there. Visit the future and write down what you see and feel. Begin to see it now, and you will begin to bring it into existence. Heaven is where God is, and God is manifested by you. God is love, and when you see what love desires, you will begin to bring what love sees into existence. This is how we bring heaven to earth and make all things new. This is how God created everything. She first saw it, then brought it into being. Did you know you are made in his image and likeness? I can't stress the importance of this action. I guarantee that if you do this, your entire life will be revolutionized. If you forget everything else in this book, don't forget this.

Although you may have dreams and intentions for the future that you are moving toward, you are not simply trying to "arrive" at some future destination where you will finally live for a living. You are actually living for a living right now. Can you see it? It's a matter of perspective. You have arrived to right now, and it's important to drink the nectar of now. Having intentions for the future without attachment to a future outcome is vitally important. Whenever we attach to something, we can rest assured that fear of not arriving at our desired intention is what is causing us to try to manipulate our intentions into reality. Attachments to future intentions blind us to the flow of life that is happening in the present tense. It's a result of being fixated on making a desired future come to pass. Attachments to a future expectation almost always cause the very thing we fear to manifest because it is the fear of an unfulfilled future desire that is driving the attachment. This fear becomes our focus, blinding us to the present. All events are simply the continuation of the present. Trying to skip over the present to arrive at a future destination is insane. When the "future" arrives, it's always in the present that we will experience it. Attachment is not necessary. Our future intentions will manifest as we are conscious of them in the present without attaching to them.

Again, there are practical things we can do in the present that can help us make the transition from the economy of survival to the economy of love.

First, we can embrace the elegance of simplicity. I can tell you from personal experience that life feels much lighter, and more beautiful, the more focused our attention is. The more possessions we possess, the more those possessions require a measure of energy from us. The less things we have, the less our attention is diverted toward those things and the more focused our attention can be toward love.

Make an active list of all the ways you are currently being sustained in life. Make an active list of your blessings. Seek to add to this list daily. At the end of each week, read this list in its entirety.

Consider sharing your living space. Rent or mortgage is often the largest expense that a person has. If living space can be shared, that's less money that is needed for this expense per person or couple. Since the need for more money often means more time that needs to be spent acquiring more money, the less money we need means the more time we will have to truly live into our true purpose. If you have space in your home, consider sharing this living space with another, or consider becoming a roommate with someone else. Sharing living expenses reduces the pull that the economy of survival has on us significantly.

Look for ways to let go of your money to invest in others. I used the word "invest" for a reason. Whenever someone invests resources, it is for the purpose of multiplication. Love, by its very nature, is reproductive. When we invest in others from the place of love, the ripple effects are eternal. If your work naturally generates steady income, consider how you can invest in others who are involved in the creative realm where income is not as steady.

Refuse to take a job simply for the money or because you are in a bind financially. Always ask how a particular job flows with your deepest desires and passion before taking it. Observe the tension this produces in your life, but do not engage the thoughts of lack as this will produce fear of the immediate future. The tension you sense when doing this is the wall that must be transcended in order to enter the present tense. When you enter the present, you will notice that everything you need in the moment is actually being provided. The more you "feel" secure, the more you will be able to perceive your own heart and what is needed instead of reacting to a sense of lack.

In anything you do, seek to serve and add value to the lives of others and to the wider world around you before you consider any other motivation for your work. If you are not sure if your work will add value and love to others, become conscious of what may be motivating you in your work.

As this book comes to a close, I would like to remind you of your mortality. No, not in a morbid or fearful way, but in a way that puts things in perspective. Many of the things we have been trained to think of as important are really not. Keeping our mortality in mind can help keep things in perspective. You have been sent here to accomplish a vitally important task. Your true work is an extension of your being which means your work is an expression of love as love is the image and likeness of the God in whose image you've been created. The work you've been sent here to do will alter the world permanently for the cause of love. There never has been a more significant life than your life. When you are truly free to love through your life's work, you will find yourself indeed living for a living.

Many voices. One message.

FREE TO LOVE
COACHING

Moving from the lie of lack to a life of love.

The purpose of Free To Love Coaching is to equip people to live a deeply fulfilling life of giving and receiving extravagant love.

To get started on this incredibly powerful journey of self-discovery, visit **www.freetolovecoaching.com**.

HERETIC HAPPY HOUR

Burning questions, not people.

Heretic Happy Hour is an unapologetically irreverent, crass, and sometimes profound conversation about the Christian faith. Hosts, Matthew Distefano, Jamal Jivanjee, and Keith Giles pull no punches and leave no stones unturned. For some serious sacred cow-tipping, there's nothing better than spending an hour of your time with us.

www.heretichappyhour.com

CPSIA information can be obtained
at www.ICGtesting.com
Printed in the USA
FSHW010028050819
60708FS